Beyond the Personality

The beginner's guide to enlightenment

Beyond the Personality
The beginner's guide to enlightenment

by
The Implicate Technology Centre

The Implicate Technology Centre
London

First published in the United Kingdom in 1987 by
The Implicate Technology Centre
BCM – ACT
London WC1N 3XX

British Library Cataloguing in Publication Data

Implicate Technology Centre

Beyond the personality : the beginner's
guide to enlightenment.
1. Mysticism
I. Title
149'.3 BL625

ISBN 0-9511839-0-7

Typeset, printed and bound in the United Kingdom by
A. Wheaton & Co. Ltd, Exeter.

The Implicate Technology Centre has been formed to meet the extensive and as yet unfulfilled need for self-help books of a secular nature, which explain in clear, direct, everyday terms what enlightenment is and how it can be attained.

Beyond the Personality: the beginner's guide to enlightenment is based on the experience of enlightened individuals living and working as ordinary people in and around London. They have pooled their experience to provide this teaching, so that others can know the benefits of enlightenment.

This book tackles the opportunity created by the current explosion of interest in enlightenment, through the use of secular language and imagery to explore issues which are normally the province of religions.

This teaching of a systematic and coherent secular system of meditation leading to enlightenment, will be completed with the publication of *The advanced guide to enlightenment*. That book is scheduled for publication in late 1987 by The Implicate Technology Centre.

Contents

Preface

The meaning of life is : life is.

The fulness of this can only be understood through experiencing the unity that is reality. This understanding through experience is not possible within the terms of your ordinary, day-to-day awareness. The first and most difficult step along the path to understanding is to attain the state of awareness known as the psychological stage of enlightenment.

This state of awareness is accessible to you if you are prepared to commit your whole being, your whole sense of purpose, to the enterprise. This book teaches any ordinary intelligent person how to experience the first or psychological stage of enlightenment within the context of ordinary, day-to-day life. This is the great adventure of the human spirit.

It is your destiny.

The Implicate Technology Centre.

1 *Introduction to implicate technology*

There is only one reality. Reality is one. All religions can be understood as models of the one reality, each relevant to particular cultures over particular time periods.

☆ ☆ ☆ ☆

What does this book teach you?

This book starts from the basis that within the natural limitations of your personality, all you can experience is your individual measure of joy and sorrow, pain and pleasure. It teaches that you will never understand the true nature of reality if you deal with people and things only through your personality, neither will you understand why your life has happened to you the way it has. This book teaches you that if you truly want to understand what your life is about, you must learn how to live beyond your personality.

This book teaches you how to attain a state of mind, tranquil and clear, which enables you to understand reality and your life in a balanced and harmonious way. You are shown how to experience directly, for yourself, that both your life and all life are only apparently separate elements in reality. You are shown how to experience for yourself that all things, all life, are in reality integrated and unified aspects of a meaningful whole: this level of experience is known as enlightenment.

Enlightenment is only possible once you learn to live beyond your personality. A simple way to achieve this is through practice of the meditation technique taught in chapter 2. Follow the detailed instructions, work to the best of your ability in the way directed, and you will travel along the path towards enlightenment.

This book for beginners teaches you how to realise the first, or psychological, stage of enlightenment with one hundred days of committed meditation practice. Psychological enlightenment is a state of mind in which you can experience a genuine and lasting detachment from emotional unhappiness. This book, then, prepares you, through the resulting peace and clarity of mind, for the advanced teachings on meditation, which lead, through experience, to a full and direct understanding of the inherent unity of reality. That state is known as the final, transcendental, stage of enlightenment.

This book teaches you how to understand reality through experience. The fruits of your experience can be expressed in religious or secular terms, according to your choice. This book is a self-help guide to experiencing the unity that is reality.

This book is entirely practical. It contains no theory. Daily practice of the simple meditation exercise, within the context explained, leads to understanding reality through experience.

Begin the journey on this path now. All the material you need is to hand in your own life. This book teaches you how to live the meaning and purpose of your life.

The key is to integrate these teachings into your ordinary, everyday life. Committed daily practice of these teachings leads to a gradual, entirely natural and harmonious transformation of your experience of life. This teaching requires no overt changes in your life, no visible markers, no new allegiances or beliefs.

Simply practise the meditation and think about your life in the context given.

☆ ☆ ☆ ☆

What is the function of the personality?

From the point of view of normal, day-to-day awareness, reality is experienced through the limitations of one's personality. The personality acts as a filter through which one interprets and understands the experiences of one's senses interacting with one's emotional, intellectual and belief structures. Each personality has its own strengths and weaknesses, its own limitations: bounded by individual limitations, one tries to understand the experience of oneself interacting with the world.

The personality encompasses the whole complex of emotions, intellectual ideas, fears, values, hopes, needs and desires which are accessible to, and form the contents of, ordinary, everyday awareness. Our well-developed psychologies teach us that each individual's behaviour is to a significant extent influenced by underlying psychological constraints. Normally, one is unconscious of one's own constraints; awareness of these underlying constraints, which determine much of one's understanding of reality, usually dawns gradually by means of the long and laborious process of maturing through time.

The key term 'consciousness' refers both to one's level of awareness at any given time and place and to the context within which this awareness operates at that time. In other words, one's level of consciousness at any time is what one is aware of, understood within the context of one's conscious and unconscious limitations. Considered objectively, each personality defines a limiting structure to the experiencing of reality.

The personality is a constraint upon one's level of consciousness. This should be reflected on carefully until it is clearly understood. Put simply, there is much more of reality which you can experience when your level of consciousness is not constrained by the personality.

☆ ☆ ☆ ☆

What, then, is reality which is both experienced and understood within the limitations of the personality?

Reality is the total of what can be known and experienced. Reality encompasses things, oneself and other people, and the manifold layers of meaning within which experience can be understood. Reality is in a constant state of flux; each moment is different from any other.

To ordinary consciousness, reality is experienced only as a state of constant flux rather than as a meaningful process. This is to say that reality is a process which includes, and interacts with, the personality. Each personality is subject to the process of reality.

☆ ☆ ☆ ☆

What are the characteristics of the interaction between one's personality and the process that is reality?

Through the complex of one's needs and desires, one attempts to live a fulfilling and satisfying life. This one achieves to a greater or lesser extent according to one's own way of measuring such matters. We all experience certain things in common. We all have our measure of joy and sorrow, physical and emotional pain and pleasure. We each have our sufferings, frustrations, disappointments and failures; our own weaknesses and fears which we face or fail to face as we are put to the test.

A common pattern of our lives is the attempt of the individual personality to attain fulfilment through the control of aspects of reality. This usually manifests itself as the wish to impose one's will on others or on oneself and the world. This is doomed to failure: we can only temporarily bend the world to our will. In the end, reality, apparently external to the needs and desires to the personality, is too powerful.

Again and again one pitches one's personality against an apparently external and uncaring world. The twin forces of one's personality and reality dance in constant opposition. In this way we waste our lives and our energies in an unwinnable struggle.

☆ ☆ ☆ ☆

Can we develop a framework, a context, in which to understand the interaction between the personality and reality?

Such a framework can be established, but not by the traditional Western technique of presenting a structured argument which states its premises, develops its reasoning based on these premises, then leads to its logical conclusion. Any such intellectual approach is inadequate to the task of understanding reality. Understanding can only be based on experience; the function of the intellect is to assist in organising one's understanding of experience, nothing more and nothing less.

Instead, the traditional Eastern technique of starting with a presentation of the central point will be used. A function of this book is to provide a teaching, the practice of which will lead to an understanding through experience of the central point or goal. When the practical instructions are followed and the framework within which the consequent experiences unfold is understood, then, at one's own pace and in one's own way, understanding will develop.

The central point, the goal of the teaching, is to achieve an understanding through experience that: reality is a process which devours the personality. The personality is a defence against the corrosive effects of reality on the ego, the limiting and relatively illusory sense of the individual 'I'.

To understand the truth of this requires a perspective, located outside the constraints of the personality, on one's life experiences, which are an integral part of reality. To attain this perspective, one's focus of awareness must move, quite naturally and at one's own pace, from the individual ego-based constraints of the personality to the freedom of the transpersonal self. When the focus of awareness settles in the self, the resulting serenity, clarity and quiet joyousness is the psychological state known as enlightenment.

Once the psychological stage of enlightenment has been reached, many aspects of the personality are understood in a different light. Gradually, one comes to realise that the experiences of one's life have taken place within a meaningful context. All one's experiences and sufferings are now understood to have a purpose; but it should be kept in mind that the understanding of meaning and purpose after the psychological enlightenment is different in nature from any such understanding held in the context of normal consciousness.

☆ ☆ ☆ ☆

What does it mean to say, 'reality is a process which devours the personality'?

To understand this, it is necessary to develop a point of view, a way of seeing the objective nature of the interaction between the personality and reality. Within the context of the personality, one's experiences and insights are subjective; however powerful, intense or varied in joy and suffering they may be, they are, in the end, personal and subjective. Viewed objectively, from a transpersonal point of view, the function of the process which is reality is to bring each individual consciousness to an awareness of its true nature.

From a focus of awareness rooted in the context of the personality, i.e. within normal consciousness, one's life is experienced in terms of the extent to which one achieves a balance between the satisfaction and lack of satisfaction of one's needs and desires. To remain locked in such a low level of consciousness is to be subject, without release, to the endless play of opposites. One experiences constantly the conflicting tensions of emotions, desires and objective reality.

Just as time devours the physical body in the course of its passage from youth through physical maturity to the gradual physical decay leading to death, so too does reality, through the passage of time, lead the personality from the innocence of childhood, past the idealism of youth and the draining realisations of life's harsh realities in maturity, to the emptiness and fear of an old age unprepared for death. A consciousness shaped by the constraints of the personality fears profoundly the transpersonal, which is, correctly, sensed as inimical to the ego, or sense of the individual self.

This, then, is what is meant by saying 'reality devours the personality':

One who remains rooted in the personality is fated to suffer the endless conflicting tensions of desire and non-fulfilment of desire. Driven by the ego-based desires of the personality, one fears that dissolution of the sense of 'I' which is the hallmark of the transpersonal. This is commonly found in the individual's fear of death. One is devoured by constant conflict and fear; in the end, one dies unfulfilled, empty, unprepared and fearful of death.

☆ ☆ ☆ ☆

Is this suffering necessary?

For one whose level of consciousness is confined within the constraints of the personality, such suffering is both inevitable and necessary. It is the product of inescapable natural laws which govern our lives as much as do the physical laws explored so thoroughly by our explicate Western technologies. Whether or not one believes in these implicate laws is irrelevant to their domination of the shape and structure of our lives. Just as the decay of the physical body is inevitable, so too is the suffering experienced within the constraints of the personality.

How can you escape from the endless cycle of psychological suffering and fear of death?

This is possible through following a path which leads to the movement of the focus of awareness from the personality-confined ego to the transpersonal self. Such a path is laid out in practical detail in this book. It is attainable by ordinary people regardless of their economic or social position in society or the circumstances of their lives.

In following the practical path detailed in this book, it will become increasingly clear that what matters is less the events of one's life (which are the preoccupation of normal consciousness) than the way in which one reacts to these events. As one moves towards the psychological enlightenment, the obsession with the outward patterning of events gives way to a deeper concern with the content of one's life experiences. With the attainment of the psychological stage of enlightenment, the understanding of one's life circumstances and their meaning merges into a harmonious sense of wholeness.

This is a profound feeling of psychological wellbeing which transcends one's material circumstances.

☆ ☆ ☆ ☆

Is there a framework which provides us with the terms of reference adequate to the task of describing the direct experience of reality?

There is only one reality. We each experience fragments of the one reality within the constructs of our personalities. In our late-twentieth-century Western culture, we have lost sight of our cultural model of the one reality, of which our day-to-day experiences form a small but vital part.

There are many models of reality available to us today: Indian, Chinese and Tibetan Buddhism, Indian Hinduism, Chinese Taoism, Christianity, Judaism and Islam, and the old Western Mystery models of the Druids and the pre-Christian Pagans. Each model is an attempt to describe the path leading to an understanding of reality in terms appropriate to a particular culture at a particular time and place.

No one model of reality gives exclusive access to the truth. Each model reflects particular historical and cultural requirements. In the West, over the past two thousand years, our culture has been shaped by the ethical framework of Christianity. Now, for great numbers of people, the old models of reality have lost their relevance.

Yet the need to understand the fulness of reality and one's place in it remains strong. So some turn back to the old Western models and other lean hungrily towards the venerable Eastern models. Few seem to find satisfaction; the great majority just live their lives from day to day in quiet desperation with no great sense of meaning or purpose. In fact the predominant world view is the woefully inadequate mechanistic model given by our science.

The scientific model of reality denies our natural desire for wholeness. Only a committed minority find satisfaction and fulfilment in the available religious models. The simple fact is that we have no culturally relevant framework within which an ordinary intelligent person can find guidance and assistance on the path to wholeness.

This book is an attempt to provide this guidance in terms accessible to such a person. For one who follows the path taught in this book, it is possible to express the resultant experiences within the terms of any religious or spiritual model of reality. All are valid in different ways; any claims to sole access to the truth are a form of religious or spiritual egotism.

However, for the majority, the atheists, agnostics, cynics and the spiritually desperate and starving, there is at present no generally accessible and relevant model. This book points towards a beginning, no more and no less; it offers guidance on the path to wholeness and fulfilment, without requiring commitment to a particular belief structure or way of living. The starting-point is now, and all the material required is to hand in your own life.

The test of the validity of this teaching is whether you experience the growth of consciousness of reality through practice. Whether or not you believe in the teaching is irrelevant. This book offers you knowledge based on experience.

☆ ☆ ☆ ☆

By what process was this book written?

This book is based on the direct experiencing of reality by members of The Implicate Technology Centre. It explains how a simple daily exercise, practised in the context of your ordinary, day-to-day life, and understood within a relevant framework, leads to a transformation in your level of awareness.

From the vantage point of this more developed consciousness, which is accessible to everyone regardless of individual life circumstances, the central validity of the old models of reality is apparent. That is to say, each describes reality in a valid and culturally different way. This book is simply a recasting of the ancient teachings in contemporary Western cultural terms.

This book is not a new translation of books of other cultures. It is a recasting of the experience those works teach about into the ordinary language and concepts we use in the West. For those who are interested in such things, chapters 2 and 5 are based on the Chinese Taoist book, *The Secret of the Golden Flower.* Chapters 3, 4, 6 and 7 are a recasting, through the filter of experience, of the discussion on the Sidpa Bardo in the Tibetan Buddhist book, *The Tibetan Book of the Dead.* Chapter 1 is a recasting of the key message of Gautama the Buddha and many other teachers: this life leads us only to suffering unless we find a way to rise above it. Chapter 8 discusses the difficulties of having such experiences in a culture ignorant of such processes.

As an illustration of this process of recasting, consider carefully the following example:

The Secret of the Golden Flower begins with the key to the process of attaining enlightenment: "The secret of the magic of life consists in using action in order to attain non-action."[1] It elaborates this point: "The Master is further concerned that people should not miss the way that leads from conscious action to unconscious non-action. Therefore he says, the magic of the Elixir of Life makes use of conscious action in order that unconscious non-action may be attained."[2] The text goes on to say that conscious action consists in the process and product of meditation.

The final chapter underlines the significance of this. "The most important things in the great Tao are the words: action through non-action. Non-action prevents a man from becoming entangled in form and image (materiality). Action in non-action prevents a man from sinking into numbing emptiness and dead nothingness."[3]

What does all this mean? Clearly, to the authors of the book, it is a matter of profound significance. Many in the West are drawn to

---

[1] Wilhelm and Jung, *The Secret of the Golden Flower;* London, Routledge & Kegan Paul Ltd, 1965, page 21.

[2] *Ibid,* page 24.

[3] *Ibid,* pages 53 - 54.

understand the meaning of this; yet we do not have an understanding of the context within which Chinese culture produced such a discipline for living.

To establish this context, we must become aware of the differences in the technologies developed by East and West. Here in the West, we have well-developed explicate technologies; that is to say, we have developed technologies to deal with material reality; these are far beyond the explicate technologies developed in the East and the West's products are eagerly sought in the East. Because of our advanced material technologies we consider ourselves the more developed culture, we acknowledge a responsibility to help the materially poorer cultures to raise their living standards.

Just as the West has turned its best minds to technologies which help us to understand and harness the power of material reality, so too has the East turned its best minds to the development of technologies which help in understanding and harnessing the power of non-material reality. Throughout the East there are many highly advanced technologies available. In contrast to the path we in the West took, these are implicate technologies; that is to say, technologies that deal with non-material reality. The products of these technologies are eagerly sought by many in the West: for years now, there has been growing interest in implicate technology products such as the martial arts, the various systems of Yoga and Zen and other Buddhist disciplines.

It is within this context that we can begin to understand what is meant by "action through non-action". It is the product of Chinese Taoist implicate technology. Its function is to direct the consciousness of any person towards understanding how to deal with the experiences which comprise ordinary life so as to obtain the greatest fulfilment from that life.

All this can be understood by an ordinary intelligent person, but it does not yet explain what the words of the above-quoted phrase mean. We can only understand their meaning through practice in using a comparable product of Western implicate technology; such a product cannot be grasped or measured with the intellect alone. Only by incorporating such a product into one's day-to-day life can its benefits be realised. This, then, is the key to gaining fulfilment in life, expressed in Western cultural terms.

Act according to your intuition.

Don't interfere.

Just let things happen.

A fuller discussion on how to apply this product of Western implicate technology will be found in chapter 3.

☆ ☆ ☆ ☆

How do you use implicate technology products?

The function of all technologies is to make available specific products to assist us in dealing with reality. In the West we are well acquainted with the uses of the products of our explicate technologies which enable us to deal with material reality; we are all familiar to a greater or lesser extent with the uses of television, cars, computers and the myriad other products of our material technologies. We use them to enhance the material quality of our lives; we live within a consumerist ethos where the possession and use of explicate technology products is a prime concern. Yet our deepest intuitions tell us there is more to life than the consumption of material products.

The function of implicate technology products is to direct the focus of awareness inwards, to assist us in learning how to deal with the non-material aspects of reality. There are many such products available in the marketplace today; some train the body and the mind, some heal the body and mind. Many, especially those from the Eastern implicate technology systems, such as Hindu, Buddhist or Taoist yogas, take one along the path towards the psychological stage of enlightenment.

It is important to be cautious in choosing implicate technology products. In the final analysis, all products of non-material technologies lead one towards the psychological stage of enlightenment, that is to say, they lead one out of the inevitable suffering of the personality into the freedom of the transpersonal. This is the birthright of each one of us – freedom cannot be bought, it can only be earned.

In our current marketplace, there are many Eastern and Western implicate technology products available. Many of the vendors of these products require a financial commitment involving sums of money not insignificant to an ordinary person. Question closely the motives and experience of individuals or organisations seeking to exchange implicate technology skills and products for money.

The Implicate Technology Centre releases inexpensive products, in the form of mass-produced books, which require no further financial commitment for their successful use. Everything that is taught in this book has been tested through the experiences of members of the Implicate Technology Centre. There is no theory in this book, only practice.

All Implicate Technology products are used by incorporating them into your daily life. Their primary function is to direct the focus of awareness inwards towards a true understanding of one's own nature. It is only by attaining the psychological stage of enlightenment that you can begin the long journey we each must travel in seeking to set ourselves in a harmonious balance with the process that is reality.

This book is used by carrying out the simple practical instructions in chapter 2. The remaining chapters are read and re-read until one is familiar with the framework. Read the book at least once consecutively, then in any order you wish.

At different times, as your work develops, different chapters will take on significance, according to the needs of the moment. This is an indication of where, in the process of moving towards the psychological enlightenment, you are at any given time. This book functions as a self-help guide in the process of transformation of awareness.

The directions are simple to read, but very demanding to apply in practice. The fruits of this teaching, freedom from the endless cycle of suffering and the fear of death, are available to anyone willing to commit their whole being to the enterprise. The price of enlightenment is no less than this.

2 *The self-help technology*

Why should anyone bother to practice meditation?

The practice of meditation has been a prime feature of many models of reality. In Eastern cosmologies or worldviews it is a practice of paramount importance; in our Western models of reality it features either directly as meditative practices or indirectly as a highly focused form of prayer. In both Eastern and Western models, meditation and what we in the West know as prayer are often closely interwined.

Clearly, in the past, meditation and prayer have been highly significant and valuable forms of activity when operating within the context of a given model of reality. The committed Muslim or Hindu or Buddhist or Christian has had meditative or prayer practices to turn to as a support in the difficulties of living. Our late-twentieth-century Western culture, however, is primarily secular in nature.

The vast majority no longer acknowledge the power and authority of the mainstream religious models of reality, yet a phenomenon of recent years has been the successful import into our Western cultures of meditative systems from the Eastern models of reality. Many have turned to meditation seeking simple benefits such as release from the stress which is such a major feature of our lives, or as a form of self-healing. Many turn to meditation within the context of a specific model of reality in an effort to understand the meaning of their lives.

All of this is a testament to the enduring power of meditation or prayer in people's lives, but it does not explain why, in a secular culture, one should bother to practise meditation.

The majority of people in our culture do not accept the comfort of the existing models of reality. That is to say, most people cannot relate the teachings of the major religions to the deep and unarticulated core of their lives. In general, our lives are lived and understood within the impoverished framework of our mechanistic worldview.

To provide purpose and meaning in our lives, a way must be found to learn to understand the true nature of how we each interact with reality. This is the purpose and function of implicate technology. It is a practical self-help technology, available to anyone in any circumstances.

To ask why one should bother to practice meditation is to ask: what is the relevance of implicate technology for me?

We live in a culture which places us increasingly under stress. The forces which shape our lives are moving increasingly out of the individual's control. We are all, to a greater or lesser extent according to our individual life circumstances, subject to the power and influence of politicians, unions, corporate and state institutions, terrorists, etc., a vast complex of social, economic, political, moral and personal pressures. We each need to learn to accept, to endure, to change and to effect change according to our circumstances.

In addition to these forces, we are subject to natural laws. Some of these laws, such as the law of gravity, are well understood by our explicate science; others, although well understood and expressed in Eastern models of reality, are barely glimpsed by our explicate sciences. Each of us must live our lives subject also to these forces.

Within this vast network of implicate and explicate forces, we each must act out our lives. None is exempt from this. These are the forces which comprise both our day-to-day lives and the deeper context which many of us intuitively sense is reality.

Within this context, we each must live out our lives and face our deaths. How does one make sense of one's individual life? How does one gain sufficient independence from these apparently overwhelming forces to live out one's life with a sense of freedom?

The purpose of implicate technology is to equip the individual with the skills necessary to attain this degree of freedom, and the understanding of how to use them. This is a state of freedom in which one has the capacity to remain clear, serene and quietly joyous regardless of external circumstances. This is the state of mind in which one is set face to face with reality.

☆ ☆ ☆ ☆

What does it mean for one to be set face to face with reality?

From the point of view of ordinary daily consciousness, one

experiences reality through the limitations and constructs of the personality. Within the framework of the personality, one enacts the experiences of one's life and death. Through the development of the personality, one moves from the naive idealism of youth to the mature awareness of life's harsh realities.

Inevitably, in the course of one's life, one experiences sorrow, pain, misery, grief and despair. This is a natural consequence of experiencing reality through the limitations of the personality. Reality devours the personality.

The inevitable suffering of one's life is a consequence of not being set face to face with reality. Only by experiencing reality directly, face to face, can one escape the cycle of suffering and fear of death. The simple meditation taught in this chapter is an Implicate Technology product structured to enable ordinary intelligent people to face reality directly.

For one whose focus of awareness is centred on the personality, suffering is inevitable. Release from this suffering can only be found through a natural shift of one's focus of awareness to the transpersonal self. Daily practice of this meditation, coupled with committed efforts to integrate its results into one's ordinary life, leads to the first, or psychological, stage of enlightenment.

Through the use of this implicate technology product, one learns how to focus the thoughts simply and clearly on one thing at a time. This is the essential skill one must develop to enable one to be set face to face with reality. Although the practice is simplicity itself, the difficulty of achieving success is not to be underestimated.

Implicate technology applied consistently over sustained periods of time and understood within a practical context transforms one's awareness of reality. The simple meditation technique taught in this chapter develops the single most important feature of any meditative system. This is the ability to focus the thoughts consistently and continuously on one object, aim, thought or experience at a time.

☆ ☆ ☆ ☆

What is the tool for the transformation of awareness and how does one use it?

Just as each human body shares a common physical anatomy, so, too, do we share a common non-material anatomy. This common structure we share extends beyond our psychological make-up. This cannot be understood by reading about the subject, or by being told, it can only be understood by direct experience.

The purpose of any structured meditative system is to direct consciousness along the path towards understanding through experience.

Although there is a great deal of interest growing in the West about using, understanding and realising the benefits of Eastern meditative systems, they are not generally appreciated in terms of their full cultured potential. In part, this is because they are implicate technology products stemming from cultures which have developed expertise in articulating certain key aspects of reality far beyond the present level of understanding in our Western cultures. This is expressed most clearly in the uses of the terms *chi* and *prana* in the Hindu, Buddhist and Taoist implicate technologies.

Anyone who has even a cursory knowledge of Eastern meditative systems will have come across these terms generally translated as 'breath' or 'life force'. The aspects of reality to which these words direct one's awareness will gradually become clear through practice of the meditation taught in this chapter. To help in understanding, you should be aware that *prana* is also known as intuition.

In Tibetan Buddhist implicate technology, intuition can also be understood as 'quick knowing'. The consistent daily practice of the meditation taught here, with a full commitment to understanding, will lead to the awakening of your intuitive faculties. As your intuition develops, so will your understanding of these teachings unfold.

To begin from the viewpoint of ordinary consciousness: we experience the material world through the five senses – to our senses, the material world is solid and real. For centuries, we in the West have relied on our sciences to aid us in understanding physical reality. In pursuing an understanding of physical reality, twentieth-century quantum physics sought to establish the existence of fundamental particles of matter. After all, everyone knows that matter is solid and so must be composed of particles uniting to form trees, bodies, hills, etc.

Here our science discovered a characteristic of material particles which is at odds with the everyday experience of our senses. Quantum physics has established that matter occurs both as particles and as waves – in other words, matter is both solid (as our five senses tell us) and not solid (which is not at all apparent to common sense).

On the one hand, we experience physical reality as actual and solid; on the other hand, our most advanced science tells us that matter is somehow both solid (particles) and a form of energy (waves). Our science has established that physical reality is not as it appears to our senses. How, then, are we to experience the true nature of reality if not through the five senses?

Each one of us possesses the latent capacity to understand the true nature of reality through the experience of a form of thought which we know in the West as intuition. This is also known in the West as the sixth sense. The function of meditation is to develop this sixth sense, a truer and more reliable experience of reality than that afforded by the other five.

To understand how meditation works to achieve this requires both continuous practice in meditation and a framework in which to place the experience as it unfolds through time.

Firstly, begin with the practice. The simplest form of meditation is to concentrate on one's own breath. All that is required is seclusion for a minimum of fifteen minutes daily.

One sits upright, in any comfortable position, focuses the eyes on the bridge of the nose, or on an object five to six feet away, and counts both the duration and frequency of the breaths. If this is too difficult, it will be sufficient to count the frequency of the breathing. Typically, we breathe about seventeen times a minute – as the practice of meditation develops through time the frequency of breathing drops gradually down to roughly once a minute.

All this is very simple to say but very hard to achieve, as anyone who has tried meditation will acknowledge. The key to achieving the considerable rewards of meditation is an accessible framework within which one can understand and develop the experiences of thought during meditation.

Secondly, then, consider the framework. To ordinary consciousness, the primary experience of thought is of a continuous web. Whirling around in awareness, sometimes faster and sometimes slower, always the continuous stream of thought is there.

The aim of meditation is to slow the stream of thoughts; this process, as it develops through time and practice, to be integrated into day-to-day life, leads to great changes in awareness. One develops the capacity for a different type of thought – intuition, or true thought. As the capacity for insight develops, one's awareness of the true nature of reality develops concurrently in a profoundly satisfying way.

The central task for anyone seeking to gain the benefits of meditation is to learn to slow the thoughts. This cannot be done by thought itself. An intellectual approach is inadequate to the task.

How, then, is one to gain control over one's thought? This is to be done through the breath. There is an intimate link between breathing and thought.

Each breath we take is accompanied by a thought. This is a process apparently without end. We cannot influence thought directly but we can influence thought through influencing the breathing.

As the breathing slows in meditation, so, too, does the flow of thoughts decrease. As this happens, true thoughts, which have continuity in themselves, begin to become accessible to consciousness. As this process develops, one's awareness of reality transforms slowly, naturally and wonderfully.

The key to meditation, then, is to focus one's awareness on one's breathing. This is by no means a simple task to sustain for even fifteen minutes daily. When one starts meditation, the thoughts are in a whirl.

One is preoccupied with the awareness of the physical surroundings and one's own comfort. One is driven to think of emotional concerns, the problems of the day and intellectual concerns. The hardest thing to achieve is the task of concentrating solely and simply on one's breathing.

How then are we to achieve this control over the breathing? For the process to succeed, the transformation must take place at a gradual, natural pace. One is not to force the breathing to be slow.

The breath should flow in through the nose, into the lungs, then deep into the abdomen, quietly and easily. The breath should flow out of the nose easily and naturally. The mouth remains closed, the teeth lightly clenched and the tongue touching the roof of the mouth.

This last is most important: the tongue acts as a connector to allow the full flow of the body's energies. This can be formally studied, for example, in Taoist or Hindu esoteric yoga. It will also occur quite naturally if no attention is paid to the process.

All that remains to explain is the hardest task: how to concentrate the thoughts on the flow of breath.

Meditation is very hard to master, but very easy to sustain once mastery has been achieved. The major area of difficulty is distraction.

This takes two common forms and the differences between them are best understood as they occur in practice.

Theoretical knowledge of meditation has little value; meditation can only be understood through experience. One is in seclusion, seated comfortably in the posture described above, trying to focus one's thoughts on the awareness of breathing, and inevitably one is distracted. As said above, this can take two main forms, both of which are a variety of laziness.

The first area of difficulty which may be encountered during meditation is sleepiness. This represents a form of distraction of which one is substantially unconscious. Quite simply, one dozes off.

The cure for this is also very simple: get up and walk around for a little. This is very important. On no account should one take the lazy option and fall asleep. The key lies in focusing the thoughts, not in diffusing them.

The second area of difficulty is distraction through fantasy. This refers to any chain of thought which occurs to distract one from awareness of one's breathing. Such chains of fantasy can be based on a myriad of initial thoughts – sexual desire, financial concerns, emotional or relationship difficulties, an event of the day, etc.

The list is endless, and the attractions of fantasy are very great. Meditation affords many opportunities to indulge in self-satisfying fantasies. One is easily tempted to follow through such chains of thought.

All such chains of thought, such fantasies, are to be resisted vigorously and with discipline. They are all, without exception, illusory, regardless of how important the subject matter is to the person meditating. Distraction through fantasy is easier to deal with than sleepiness; this is because, with discipline, one can become aware of the distraction and so exercise self-control. The discipline is simply to bring one's awareness back to one's breathing.

All the problems which crop up are a function of distraction or laziness. They may manifest as fantasies, sleepiness or laboured breathing. The two cures are straightforward, either walk around a little until the mind is settled or focus the thoughts on one's breathing.

Persistent daily practice for a minimum of fifteen minutes brings success, through time.

As one develops in the process of freeing the mind from illusory distractions, so, gradually, it becomes possible to focus the thoughts on one's breathing. The full benefits of meditation can only be realised through rhythmical breathing, natural and uncontrolled. One begins by counting both the length of one's breaths and their frequency; equally one sits quite still with eyes focused on the nose, or five to six feet in front – this is an aid to concentration, nothing more.

As one develops in the practice of meditation, success can be measured in the rate of breathing. Once the level of breathing slows to four times a minute or less, the benefits become significant on many levels. Gradually, there comes a complete transformation of one's experience of daily living, easily, spontaneously and wonderfully.

This is known in all spiritual systems, or models of reality, as a transformation of consciousness. For those able to dedicate all of their energy, intelligence and concentration to the process of meditating daily, the transformation of consciousness can be effected within one hundred days. This teaching is based on the experience of the Implicate Technology Centre in using this meditative practice.

Since we in the West know so little of the transformation of consciousness, which is the natural goal for each one of us, we lack both the framework and the terms of reference to articulate the experience. This, in part, is why it is difficult to describe the successful experience of meditation. Nonetheless, the benefits are substantial and indeed, in their full significance, immeasurable.

Whilst these benefits cannot be spelled out, pointers can be provided for a consciousness experiencing them, giving a framework within which to understand them. This is to be found in observing the passage of thoughts during meditation. After a time, when the work has begun to develop and mature, it becomes possible to experience the following.

One learns to focus the attention on one's breathing, and is able to monitor its duration and frequency. At the same time, one has learnt to halt the flow of fantasy, to end a particular stream of thought at will. One is sitting quite still, the breathing quiet, relaxed and natural, and one is able to move the attention from the breathing to the stream of thoughts at will.

This is a position of great ambiguity, and many wonderful experiences are possible in this state. It is very difficult to concentrate on the breathing for sustained periods; always the thoughts drift off. Equally if one exercises self-discipline and ends the stream of fantasy by becoming aware of what one is thinking, it is very hard to restrict the thoughts to one's breathing.

In that experience of pivoting between arid fantasy and pure clarity of awareness of breathing lies the seed of profound transformation of consciousness. If one continues in this practice of alternating between simple awareness of the present moment and exercising conscious control over the flow of thoughts by simply ending the current thought, one gradually becomes aware of a different type of thought. This is a product of the sixth sense, insight or intuition.

These thoughts are quite different from the thoughts of ordinary consciousness. They are not a reflection on reality, as are ordinary thoughts; rather they are a direct experiencing of reality. Consciousness and reality are in the process of integrating.

These thoughts are an organic part of reality. They reflect an awareness of reality in a particular consciousness, in a form appropriate to the level of clarity and terms of reference of that person at that place and time. The experience of these thoughts can be couched within any religious or spiritual framework; equally it is accessible to those who operate without such a framework, such as atheists or agnostics.

☆ ☆ ☆ ☆

This, then, is the process which leads to the unfolding of true thoughts. This transformation of consciousness is a wonderful experience. One becomes aware of so much more. This experience is impossible to convey in words. Simply, one begins to understand.

To attain this, you must learn how to transform your life through the experience of meditation. The key to this is deceptively simple. Once again it is easy to read and hard to put into practice.

When understood in practice, through day-to-day experience, it becomes a wonderfully easy way to operate in harmony with reality. This, then, is the key to using the skills gained in meditation to transform your day-to-day experience of life, and expand your awareness of reality.

Act according to your intuition.

Don't interfere.

Just let things happen.

☆ ☆ ☆ ☆

☆ ☆ ☆ ☆

3 *Characteristics of the period prior to the psychological stage of enlightenment*

How do you measure your progress along the path towards the psychological stage of enlightenment?

Reality can be understood either as a mechanical, or as an organic, process – an infinite and a unified whole. Everything that happens within reality has meaning. The first and most difficult step along the path to understanding reality through experience is to grow and expand your awareness until it stabilises in the psychological state known as the first stage of enlightenment.

Reality is an organic machine structured to operate in accordance with immutable laws. To understand and experience reality as it is, your actions must be in harmony with the natural laws which govern and inform all that can be experienced. Each one of us is an integral and organic component of reality.

Reality is an infinite process unfolding through time, configured to operate at one setting only. The past is memory, individual or cultural, the future is both potential and fantasy: always and unendingly the process occurs *now*. As you move towards the psychological stage of enlightenment, through the practice of meditation, progress can be measured by the extent to which you interpret your day-to-day experiences within the context of what is happening now, at this present moment.

Karma is a term used in Eastern implicate technology systems to describe one of the implacable laws of reality. Your karma is the result of the choices you make. In the West, we know karma as the law of cause and effect.

Psychologically, our culture understands this unyielding law as the accumulated weight of experience, preserved within oneself, and shaping one's choices and experiences. The traditional teaching of our deeper psychologies involves a tortuous process of gradually understanding and coming to terms with these deep psychological determinants which shape each individual's behaviour. The teachings offered here show a well-trodden and faster path to freedom from the accumulated weight of experience which shapes each moment experienced in ordinary states of awareness.

As each of us ages and matures, the weight of our burdens increases. In our highly stressful culture, day-to-day life becomes an increasing struggle. Consistent, committed daily practice of this meditation leads to a profoundly fulfilling release from the sense of burden.

The key to releasing the full benefits of meditation lies in understanding the occurrences of your day-to-day life in terms of these teachings. This is the raw beginning of the fundamental process of learning to live your life in meditation. This meditation is a simple self-help tool available to anyone committed to transforming her or his daily experience of living.

The key to effecting the transformation within oneself is very easy to learn, but very hard to apply. The meditation teaches you to focus your concentration on one simple activity. The key is always to understand each moment of each day in terms of these teachings – always to keep the teachings in mind.

To effect the transformation successfully within a hundred days, you need a context within which you can operate meaningfully, to guide you through the many choices you make each day. To attain the psychological stage of enlightenment you need give your allegiance to no force outside yourself. Remember the teachings within the context of Act:

Act according to your intuition

Set face to face with reality, when you are experiencing reality directly, each moment offers you a choice. As you choose or fail to choose, so you create your karma. Follow the still small voice of your intuition.

Don't interfere

Each one of us is an integral and organic component of reality. By interfering, you choose to act against the flow of reality. Allow reality to unfold both within yourself and externally.

Just let things happen

To live in the flow of reality is to experience your life with clarity, serenity and a quiet fulfilling joy. This is the path to integrating your awareness into reality – this is the path to experiencing your life in the fulness of reality. Learn to accept reality as it unfolds.

This teaching on Act is the key to the process of enlightenment, the secret of the golden flower. To live in accordance with these teachings is to experience your life as a dynamically unfolding process. But first you must learn to be passive in the face of reality. Learn actively to accept your ordinary day-to-day reality in its utter fulness.

The measure of how close you are to attaining the psychological stage of enlightenment is the extent to which you are able to understand the experiences of your life in the terms of these teachings while fitting your behaviour within the constructs of Act. As you develop, your intuitive awareness of time will unfold – you will gradually lose the illusory sense of past, present and future; gradually you will gain the ability to live in the ever-present now. Finally, you will be free from the burden of the past, free at last from the psychological burdens which you have carried for so long.

☆ ☆ ☆ ☆

Live
Live the teachings,
live the teachings.

Act
Act according to your intuition.
Don't interfere.
Just let things happen.

The formula for attaining enlightenment is:

Throughout your life, Live and Act

☆ ☆ ☆ ☆

What is it like to experience life on the path to the psychological stage of enlightenment?

Although each of us is born, lives and dies, the experiences of each life are unique. Similarly, although the mechanics of the path to the first enlightenment are common to all, each of us experiences the path in a different way. In our spiritually barren Western cultures, the path to the psychological enlightenment is challenging, often difficult and sometimes dangerous.

As you develop in understanding, according to your gifts and temperament, so you will seek to articulate the unfolding of reality in the terms of your worldview. You may choose to articulate your experience in the religious terms of mainstream Christianity, Judaism or Islam; or you may be inclined towards the spiritual models of the Jewish Kabbala, Islamic Sufism, Western Paganism or the higher teachings of Hinduism, Buddhism or Taoism. Equally, in our largely secular Western cultures, you may be an atheist or an agnostic.

Your belief structure determines how you understand and articulate your experience of reality. All belief structures act as a distorting mechanism on the clear understanding and experiencing of reality. This teaching of the clear setting face to face with reality offers knowledge based on experience. No belief structure is required – simply practice the teachings.

Even the atheist and agnostic have belief structures, we all do. Learn to be guided not by beliefs, but by what you know and understand through direct experience. Your beliefs are an impediment on the path to understanding; what matters is that you directly experience reality.

As you experience reality directly, you will seek to articulate your understanding in the terms of a belief structure relevant to your needs. You can choose with equal validity to follow a religious or a secular path. All models of reality reflect reality according to the varying needs of the cultures, times and individuals which produce and utilise them.

Although all models of reality are valid in different ways and in different cultural environments, do not expect to find that the representatives of these models are trained to understand and deal with the issues raised in this book. Priests, ministers and rabbis are ordinary individuals trained in theological and religious matters. Their training does not, in general, provide them with a path towards understanding reality through experience.

As you experience the difficulties of the continuous emotional transformations necessarily involved, you may be tempted to turn to the medical profession for guidance and assistance during this period of uncertainity in your life. Be extremely cautious in approaching a profession which is trained to understand and treat the human body as separate parts. These people are unlikely to be trained in the skills of treating a person experiencing the transformations leading to wholeness.

Become aware of the alternative therapies available. Many of these involve inexpensive treatment of the whole person. As you become sensitive to your own needs, you will be drawn to an appropriate source of healing.

In the spiritually advanced cultures of the East, it is traditional to be taught this process of the gradual transformation of awareness directly by a living, recognised master. Our Western cultures have developed on the sound basis of the Judeo-Christian code of ethics. In the current spiritually barren cultural conditions, it is unlikely that you will be taught in the traditional face to face manner by a living teacher. In general, you will have to develop, through practice of the skills taught in this book, the ability to survive, flower and transform, in a culture which is inimical and hostile to the process of inner development.

Finally, do not anticipate understanding or help from your family or friends. It is possible that through their lack of understanding of the process you are experiencing they will react with incomprehension, hostility and fear. Through practice of the day-to-day adaptation and survival skills taught in chapter 8, you will, in time, find the living guidance, support and companionship you truly need and deserve.

☆ ☆ ☆ ☆

How does one experience the uncertainty of being set face to face with reality?

As you develop in understanding, through the experience of integrating the fruits of meditation into your everyday life, you enter into a period of increasing uncertainty. Your previously held beliefs about what is important and real crumble in the face of direct experience of reality. However disconcerting, unpleasant and miserable you find this experience, remember it is a necessary and healing part of the process of becoming set face to face with reality.

This state of uncertainty is a necessary process of eroding and dismantling, through your reaction to the circumstances of your life, the belief structures underpinning your personality. The structures you have imposed on reality, the way your beliefs have shaped your thoughts and actions, are being dissolved in the face of reality. Reality devours the personality.

This process heals through removal of the illusory limitations of the personality. This natural, painful and difficult experience leads to your awareness stabilising, in time, beyond the personality. It is only when one's awareness operates outside of emotional and intellectual structures that the true setting face to face with reality can begin.

The feelings of misery and sorrow which occur now are the birth pangs of your new awareness. Like natural childbirth, the experience becomes more fulfilling when one learns to detach oneself from the pain. Gradually, as you endure through time, you will experience a new understanding, a release from pain into clarity, serenity and quiet joyousness.

The uncertainty of this period, as the illusory structures of the personality are swept away, leads to a profound sense of instability. The difficulties and dangers of this stage can be compounded if those with whom one is accustomed to share one's life are unaware of, or hostile to, the process of inner transformation. The way to emerge from these difficulties in your life is to Live and Act.

If you seek to interfere, in your distress, you will only gain more trouble. Learn to accept without interference the events of your life as they unfold. Above all, learn to develop your sense of empowering your life only by following your intuition.

At this time, your life as you have understood and experienced it will seem to be dissolving in uncertainty. Learn not to seek to impose your own sense of order on reality. Put aside your desire for stability and security in your life.

Through daily practice of the meditation in the context given, you will gradually develop a profound sense of inner stillness and security. Gradually, you will learn to accept the conditions of your life without interfering. Above all, learn to shape your life actively, in accordance with the natural laws governing reality, by becoming centred in the midst of conditions.

Throughout your life, Live and Act. There are no circumstances or conditions, no hazards of life, which cannot be harmoniously negotiated through practice of these skills. Rise above the circumstances of your life through becoming centred in the midst of conditions.

What does it mean, to be centred in the midst of conditions?

This is a very fine phrase: centred in the midst of conditions. It should be thought about carefully. When you understand this as a continuous experience, and not just intellectually or emotionally, you will have attained the psychological stage of enlightenment.

The conditions which constrain our lives are common to each of us, but the specific details vary according to individual circumstances. These conditions are imposed both internally within the personality, and externally upon the personality. They operate on both the material and non-material levels of reality.

There are ten conditions which interweave, waxing and waning endlessly, to form each moment you experience. The circumstances of your life are shaped by these conditions: karma; space and time; physical, emotional and intellectual limiting factors; moral and social constraints, and political and economic pressures. The purpose of the power discipline taught later in this chapter is to empower you to deal effectively with and to transform the conditions of your life.

The condition of karma is discussed in detailed contemporary terms in chapter 4. In our spiritually barren, late-twentieth-century Western cultures, we have only a slight degree of understanding of the crucially important nature of karma. Unless you are responsive to the promptings of karma in your life, you can have no hope or prospect of a genuinely fulfilling life.

Birth and death punctuate our lives. As we age, our lives unfold through understanding and experience. Time is the medium through which all things occur.

Each of our bodies requires space to exist. The things which exist through space constrain and limit us, through our needs and desires for them. Space is the medium through which all things occur.

Time and space are inextricably woven together. They are the basic conditions of existence. Every being with any form of awareness, and every thing, is subject to these dual forces.

The conditions of space and time are discussed more fully in the transpersonal meditiations of chapter 5. The full teachings on the nature of space and time are beyond the scope of this book. The final stage of enlightenment, the union of self with reality, only occurs when the unified nature of space and time has been fully realised through experience.

In our cultures, we are familiar with discussing and analysing our lives in terms of the seven remaining conditions. This chapter discusses them within the context of Implicate Technology disciplines. Practice of these disciplines will empower you to understand and break free from the oppressive forces dominating your life.

Be clear: every unenlightened person lives a life hemmed in and limited by the ten conditions – just because you are unaware of your own limitations doesn't mean that they don't exist. The purpose of these teachings is to provide you with the skills to triumph over the conditions of your life. If you confuse this with vain dreams of triumph over your opponents, then reality, through the workings of karma, will deal with such unenlightened behaviour in its own way.

In the midst of these conditions is yourself, experiencing life through action and reaction to things and people. Through practice of these teachings you will learn to focus your awareness of reality through the still, calm centre of your self. This is what it means to be 'centred in the midst of conditions'.

☆ ☆ ☆ ☆

In what way are emotions, experienced within the limitations of the personality, relatively illusory?

Prior to attaining the first stage of enlightenment, the emotions are the primary medium through which you experience the conditions of life. You respond across the range of emotions according to the way your personality interacts with reality. As the circumstances of your life unfold, so you respond emotionally to a greater or lesser degree, according to your individual nature.

It is possible for a personality to appear to operate primarily from an intellectual rather than an emotional base. This is simply a form of emotional camouflage, based on a flight from the reality of emotional experience. It is not possible to experience life fully through the intellect.

All aspects of the personality set limiting structures on the direct experiencing of reality. The emotional range of responses, as experienced within the constructs of the personality, embodies a relatively underdeveloped reaction to reality. In relation to one who experiences reality from the standpoint of the first stage of enlightenment, these emotional responses are best understood as self-generated, self-perpetuating activities, illusory in the face of reality.

The experience of time as fragmented into past, present and future becomes understood as an illusion relative to the sense of the eternal present which is experienced after attaining the first stage of enlightenment. In the same way, the emotions experienced as real within the limitations of the personality become experienced as only relatively real. After the first stage of enlightenment, emotions are still experienced within the personality, but now such emotions are understood as being of only relative and limited importance in the face of reality.

☆ ☆ ☆ ☆

How is one to deal with the experience of life in the midst of these conditions?

One's reaction at first, before practice of these teachings has borne fruit, remains as before. One acts and reacts according to the blend of emotions and the system of values held, which form the basis for the choices made by the personality at each moment. One incurs karmic consequences within the relatively illusory limitations of the personality.

As your experience of these teachings develops, you will learn new skills through the practice of meditation. At first, you will simply develop basic skills such as control of the breathing and patience. These are very valuable skills in themselves; a great deal depends on them.

It makes no difference to the realisation of the fruits of these teachings in your life whether you are unemployed or in work, poor or not. In the path to enlightenment, the absence of money no more hinders one who lacks it than its presence helps one who possesses it. All are equal in the face of reality.

As you progress in your commitment to the daily practice of meditation, the practice itself will become the central thread of your life. For this, you depend totally on yourself, you need no objects and only the simplest of conditions. This is something for yourself and completely within your own power to achieve.

You may object that not everyone can ensure time alone and uninterrupted – it is not always easy. The answer is that if you cannot create such simple conditions then there will be no enlightenment. This is very hard work, according to your life circumstances.

Once awoken, the drive towards enlightenment is strong within us. Everything else pales into unimportance beside it; yet the path to enlightenment involves all we experience. practice of these teachings will awaken your innate capacity to experience enlightenment.

Gradually, as the fruits of meditation ripen in your life, you will begin to experience the events and activities of each day with a new understanding. As your awareness goes through the many emotional transformations before the first enlightenment, you will gradually develop the ability to understand reality in a simple, clear and direct way. In the midst of conditions, you will be better able to understand, and deal with, the power structures imposed on your life.

☆ ☆ ☆ ☆

What are these power structures which influence each life so deeply?

Each one, each thing, in existence is subject to the conditions of time and space. We each, sooner or later, will experience death. We each have similar minimum requirements for physical survival.

To live our lives, we each require an adequate supply of food, drink, shelter and warmth. One way or another, we each must find a means to procure what we need and desire. In this way we are all the same.

We place a great deal of value on what we need and desire, whether people or things, explicate or implicate, experienced physically, emotionally, intellectually or beyond. Through our individual circumstances and conditions, these needs and desires shape our lives. To fulfil them, we learn to acquire, and submit to, power.

These skills in the ways of power are developed from birth, with the first demands for fulfilment. As we grow to adulthood, we learn to deal with the power structures surrounding those involved in our lives. We each, according to our willingness to understand, learn from experience who holds the power in any situation.

This holds true for all of us. All things are created through power. The more clearly you are aware how power is structured in a particular situation, the more likely you are to create a satisfying outcome.

In the final analysis, we each create the shape of our own lives, subject to the explicate and implicate laws of reality. According to the clarity of your mind, you will be more or less aware of the truth of this. Understanding your life in the context of these teachings will empower you to achieve a more fulfilling life through practice of the power discipline.

☆ ☆ ☆ ☆

What is this power discipline?

It is a way of acting, through understanding, to negotiate your way through the hazards of any particular situation. In every situation, in every set of conditions, no matter how adverse, there is always power available to you. Committed practice of the power discipline will enable you to identify and utilise the power inherent in any situation.

Preparation for the power discipline begins with daily practice of the meditation. Gradually, you will learn to incorporate the fruits of meditation into your life by Live-ing and Act-ing. In this way you learn to set yourself face to face with reality.

The more directly you are set face to face with reality, the more you see any situation clearly, as it is, the more possible it is to produce a fulfilling outcome. The power discipline reflects the harmonious laws governing reality. To use power for unselfish ends incurs positive karmic consequences, to use power for selfish ends incurs negative karmic consequences.

The law of karma will be discussed more fully in chapter 4. It is inviolable. It is inherent in the structure of reality.

Practice of this discipline will empower you to deal with any situation, through a clear understanding. As you choose, through your actions, so you shape your life. According to your motives, so you will incur the karmic consequences of your actions.

You are free to choose and to Act, now, and at all times, as best you are able in the prevailing circumstances. We are all subject to the conditions of space, time and karma. Within this context, we each must face reality.

Practice of the power discipline will help you face reality. You are free to use it unselfishly or selfishly, for good or evil, according to your nature. The power discipline is a smooth, flowing, harmonious, organic action, understood in three steps:

Input, Pivot then Act

☆ ☆ ☆ ☆

How does the Input step unfold?

The first step is the one in which the intellect is very important. Your intellect is an essential tool to help you understand reality through analysis. Remember, however, intellectual analysis is, in itself, inadequate to the task of understanding reality through experience.

You begin by becoming aware of the situation you are in. Every situation occurs within many overlapping sets of conditions. The more conditions you are aware of, the wider the context within which you understand the situation, the better you are able to deal directly with reality.

Begin with the simplest conditions. Become aware of how the power is structured and who wields it. Begin to face reality directly.

Become aware of the physical, emotional, intellectual, moral, social, political and economic conditions determining the outcome of each situation you find yourself in. All of this occurs within the context of space, time and karma. We each live our lives, as best we can, within the circumstances imposed on us by these conditions.

Begin by understanding each situation within the terms of the lessons you have learnt by the daily practice of meditation. Become aware of who holds the power and how it is wielded. Learn to identify and use your own power, and when to submit to another's.

The power analysis of the physical situation embraces all the significant physical elements. These objects, people or forces empower yourself and others in myriad ways, through legal, moral, or physical ownership. Learn to identify the nature of the power involved, who holds the power and how it is wielded. Only then will you have a clear understanding of how you stand in relation to this power.

The power analysis of the emotional situation embraces all the discernable and relevant emotions of yourself and others. These emotions arise through the complex of our needs and desires, for people and things. The more you are able to rise above the emotions of your personality, through realising their relatively illusory nature, the less will you be subject both to the power of your emotions and to other people's capacity to wield power over you through your emotional links with them or with things.

The power analysis of the intellectual situation embraces all the aspects of the experience which are susceptible to intellectual discrimination. The function of your intellect is to assist in understanding your experience, it is secondary to experience itself. The ideas of the mind are relevant to us relative to our ability to use them to attain what we need and desire.

The power analysis of the moral environment embraces all those activities and desires, concerning people and things, which operate within your own or others' moral constructs. All moral codes have power in a particular situation, according to the extent to which those present subscribe to the code. Become aware of the effects of moral conditions on your own viewpoint and that of others.

The power analysis of the social situation embraces all the frameworks of custom and law which constrain our behaviour. The power of these frameworks, in any specific situation, depends on how enforceable they are in subtle and overt ways. Become aware of the social constraints imposed on and by yourself and others.

The power analysis of the political situation embraces all the ways employed by yourself and others to gain your own ends. Politics, in the widest sense, is the process whereby individuals and groups control and manipulate, to impose their will upon others. Learn to recognise who is doing what, to whom, and why – then you will understand the politics of the situation.

The power analysis of the economic situation embraces all the conditions imposed on us by our own and others' needs and desires for material things. Control of material things is usually maintained by physical force, or through more subtle means. In any situation, learn to recognise how you are constrained by your needs and desires for material things.

These conditions interweave and combine, to a greater or lesser degree, in each situation you face. Through practice of the Input step, you will become aware of the conditions imposed on yourself and others. Be clear in your understanding of your constraints; set yourself face to face with reality.

The complexity of this process of analysis refects the complexity of your actual experience. As you first practise, Input may be time-consuming and require a great deal of thought about your life circumstances. After a time, as you become more aware, you will be able to perform the Input step with speed and fluidity.

☆ ☆ ☆ ☆

How does the Pivot step unfold?

The Input step, the process of analysis, is as complete as you are willing and able to make it. You become aware, to a greater or lesser degree according to the amount and quality of your effort, of the conditions imposed on yourself and others. You are aware of the way the power in the situation is structured.

The task of the Pivot step is to prepare for an action which will alter the balance of power, harmoniously. For an action to achieve this, it must be simple, daring and effective. Such an action can only be supplied by your intuition.

The process of analysis, through the Input step, reveals to you the configuration of conditions which shapes the environment under analysis. You are now aware of the forces, pressures and people who hold, or are subject to, power in the situation. Before you can harmomiously weave a path through all these conditions you must become still.

Be centred in the midst of conditions. Understand that your personal configuration of needs and desires is illusory relative to the implacable power structures of reality. Be still, simply understand the situation as it is, and not from the relatively illusory and selfish viewpoint of your personality.

As you become centred in the midst of conditions, your thoughts will become calm, still and clear. You will cease to understand things in terms of the satisfaction of your needs and desires. You will understand that if you act to further your personal desires, reality will devour your works – none is exempt from this process.

Poised, centred in the midst of conditions, your understanding of the situation will configure in a lightning flash of intuition. Aware of when to wield and to yield to power, your intuition will articulate your next action. This is the moment when it becomes possible to Pivot the balance of power.

☆ ☆ ☆ ☆

How does the Act step unfold?

There are ten conditions, not nine. There are ten conditions, not eleven. Every situation you are set face to face with, in reality, can be understood as configured in the terms of these ten conditions – karma; space and time; physical, emotional and intellectual limiting factors; moral and social constraints, political and economic pressures.

The Input step, the analysis of the situation, is completed. The Pivot step, the lightning flash of intuitive understanding creating the possibility of harmoniously transforming the balance of power, is completed. Now is the time to Act.

The Action you take should flow harmoniously from your circumstances. Through understanding your experience, your intuition will guide you towards the next step. Learn to act on the still, quiet, voice of your intuition.

For your Action to avoid incurring negative karmic consequences, it should not interfere with people or things. To interfere is an act of self-will and goes against the flow of reality. Reality is a harmonious, self balancing, unity; if you act against the natural flow of events you will, sooner or later, incur a corresponding negative reaction.

When you Act, just let things happen, easily and naturally, within yourself and in terms of your behaviour towards other people and things. In every situation, no matter how apparently hopeless, there is always power for you to use harmoniously. If you wield and yield to power in an organic, flowing way, reality will unfold in its own manner.

4 *The time of testing*

In what way is reality a unity?

We can only understand and live our lives fully when we experience reality as a unity. No one is exempt from this. Anything less is a life unfulfilled, except by illusory satisfaction in transient attainments.

It is beyond the scope of this book on implicate technology to guide you along the path to the final stage of enlightenment, the understanding through experience of the unity that is reality. But although this book is primarily aimed at guiding you towards the first stage of enlightenment, the basic skills it teaches, when fully developed under careful guidance, will take you all the way to the final stage of enlightenment. This chapter teaches the unity of reality from a perspective accessible to an ordinary intelligent person.

In reality, everything which happens to you, every set of circumstances you experience, forms an infinitesimal part of an inconceivable, unified whole. From the viewpoint of ordinary, everyday awareness, the conditions of life are not experienced as part of an organically unified and meaningful whole. The first step in going beyond the relatively illusory sense of individual separateness is to understand the all-embracing and unifying power of karma.

In our late-twentieth-century secular culture, we are well used to analysing everyday situations in terms of seven of the ten conditions already mentioned – physical, emotional, intellectual, moral, social, political and economic. The full teachings on space and time, understood through experience as inseparable parts of a unified whole, lie outside the scope of this book. When you understand through your everyday experience these teachings on karma, you will have gained a new way of realising the inherent richness and unity of your ordinary life.

The unified process that is reality, always unfolding now, configures each circumstance of your life with absolute love and compassion. At every moment, you are tested by karma to aid you in your development along the path towards the final enlightenment. Through these tests, karma guides you towards the next step on the path ahead.

From the perspective of ordinary day-to-day awareness, reality cannot be experienced as a coherent unity. The machine that is reality devours the works of the component personalities. These personalities operate together, according to the inherent, implacable, implicate laws, to experience the process that is reality. Within each personality, this is experienced as the suffering caused by life's difficulties.

In reality, there is only, ever, the here and now. Life is, and each moment contains infinite potential. In reality, your life is infinite in its potential for fulness.

☆ ☆ ☆ ☆

How is one to develop an understanding of the workings of karma?

Karma is one of the ten fundamental conditions influencing every situation you experience in your life. Through the workings of karma, you will come to understand the purpose and meaning of your life. Through the daily practice of meditation, you will develop the ability to harmonise your choices with the direction karma indicates for you.

One of the fruits of meditation is the development of your intuition, or sixth sense. Use this intuitive sense to develop your ability to understand the karmic implications of each situation you experience. This ability is developed through understanding life in the context of your karma.

Be clear about this: your day-to-day suffering, your ordinary distress from the pressures and complexities of your life, has meaning and purpose. The purpose of karma is this: once you have learnt the lesson karma is teaching you in each situation you experience, karma will configure the circumstances of your life so that you are able to learn the next lesson. Once you have attained the psychological enlightenment you will have the ability to move in harmony with karma.

What are the workings of karma?

Karma and unbounded compassion intertwine indistinguishably to shape every moment you experience. This compassion is not apparent within the terms of your personality, although in a religious sense, it is accessible through faith. The unified proocess which is reality, and each of its component parts, are configured to operate in profound harmony through the workings of karma, all shaped by absolute compassion.

Karma embodies the moral force inherent in reality. We are all component parts of the one reality, operating within an infinite framework of actions ocurring on many levels of reality simultaneously, yet united in meaning. Each choice you make, each action you take, operates within an implacable moral framework configured so as to direct the growth of understanding of your own nature.

All religious or secular moral codes are relatively illusory in the face of the implacable moral force governing every situation you experience. By your actions, you can lie to yourself and other people. Your lies, to yourself and others, are no secret in the face of reality.

Any action can be justified within the terms of one moral code or another. In reality, many actions you experience emotionally or morally as valid or necessary can be seen, in a wider context, as self-deceiving. Karma is the process whereby reality structures the circumstances of your life to develop the understanding of your own nature.

Reality is experienced, once the first stage of enlightenment is attained, as layer upon layer of meaning, as infinitely expanding layers of context. Actions seen as harmless in one context are understood as selfish in a wider, more enlightened context. Your karma will always direct your awareness to the next context in which you should understand your situation.

When you learn the lesson karma is teaching you, at any time in any situation, the causes of your suffering will, in time, cease to occur. When you experience the difficulties of your life as recurring patterns, that is a sign that you have not yet understood the karmic purpose inherent in your situation. When you experience the difficulties of your life as spontaneous occurrences, within a context of enlightened awareness, that is a sign that you are working in harmony with karma.

Most of your karma is generated and experienced through personal, social and economic activities. Through the actions you choose to make, the extent to which you understand your own nature is revealed in the face of reality. Reality spontaneously structures your life circumstances to direct you, through the workings of karma, to understand this or that aspect of your nature.

Your karma is a result of the choices you make. Creating negative karma results in unhappiness and suffering; creating positive karma results in opportunities to grow in the understanding of your own nature. Reality, the whole machine and its component parts, is an organic self-balancing process occurring simultaneously on many levels.

Karma is configured to test you, not you to test karma: be sensitive to the power and direction of karma in your life. Karma is more terrible than anything humanity can devise and more arousing than the gentlest caress of impassioned lovers. Always try to understand each situation you experience in terms of your karma: you are a component of reality – be willing to learn the lesson reality is teaching you at each moment.

☆ ☆ ☆ ☆

What is the time of testing?

Karma tests and guides you at each moment of your life. Every moment of your life is an opportunity to advance further along the path along which reality is guiding you. Committed daily practice of the meditation, together with these teachings, will empower you to understand the truth of this through experience: no belief is necessary, although in the initial stages it may help, according to your nature.

The tests, imposed on your life by karma, become more concentrated, more severe, as you approach the first, or psychological, stage of enlightenment. This is experienced as a period of great complexity and difficulty in your life. Committed daily practice of the meditation will empower you to resolve and leave behind the difficulties of this stage.

The purpose of this period in your life is to test your capacity to be objective about what you experience. Your primary psychological characteristic, prior to the first stage of enlightenment, is to experience reality through the filter of your emotional and intellectual projections. This emotional and intellectual subjectivity of your ordinary personality becomes understood as self-deceiving and illusory, relative to the post-enlightenment objectivity which you will attain when you have freed yourself from emotional and intellectual limitations.

These emotional and intellectual projections are to be understood in the way you see things, as coloured by your own attitudes. Learn to become aware of the reality of situations, independent of your needs and desires. The method of achieving this is committed daily practice of the meditation, understood within the context of your ordinary daily life.

Through the workings of karma, you are tested by the circumstances of your life. This is a natural consequence of your awareness moving outside your personality and towards wholeness. The circumstances of your life come together spontaneously to test how far your self-awareness has developed and how capable you are of operating with a sense of detachment from your own needs and desires.

You are being tested on your ability to operate at arm's length from the constraints of your personality. The key to release from the pre-enlightenment tension into a serene objectivity in the midst of conditions, lies in gaining detachment from the all-pervasive influence of the emotions. Practical advice on the handling of your emotions is contained in chapter 6.

☆ ☆ ☆ ☆

What is the succesful outcome of these trials?

In the words of the ancient, pre-Christian, Druidic and Pagan Western Mystery traditions you will have died and been reborn. In the Christian sense of this, your old self will have died to be reborn in the love of Jesus. In the terms of the Jewish Kabbalah, you will have obtained the intermediate state of mind of a *benoni.*

You will be an initiate who has become prepared, by enduring and triumphing over the trials of your life, for the work of developing your understanding, through experience, of the implicate links between your nature and reality. Through this work, you will come to experience that, in reality, all people and things are indivisibly intertwined and enfolded in an inexpressible unity. The function of implicate technology is to provide you with guidance, based on experience, to help you along the way.

Within the terms of implicate technology, you will have experienced a shift in consciousness, from an awareness of reality confined by the relatively illusory limitations of your personality, to a clear, serene awareness of reality, quietly rejoicing in the freedom of the transpersonal self. This will be your achievement and yours alone; the responsibility for your attaining enlightenment is yours alone; equally, if you develop unwavering determination, in the face of reality, to endure and learn through time, there are no hindrances to enlightenment which you cannot overcome. In a psychological sense, you will have realised the unconditioned state.

☆ ☆ ☆ ☆

What does it mean to realise the unconditioned state, in a psychological sense?

As taught in chapter 3, in reality, every experience of your life is bounded by a specific configuration of the ten conditions. The specific details vary from life to life, and from situation to situation. What remains constant is the influence, on your life, of these ten conditions at every moment.

The successful outcome of attaining the psychological stage of enlightenment involves transcending the relatively illusory limitations of your personality. Put simply, you go beyond your emotional and intellectual conditioning. You are able to exist, in your daily life, in a state unconditioned by your previous emotional and intellectual constraints.

This is a state of clarity, serenity and quiet joy, where you are centred in the midst of conditions, becoming increasingly free of the thrall of your needs and desires, accepting reality as it unfolds to your awareness. The world is as full as ever of people and things you need and desire; only now you become increasingly freed to react or not, in any situation, according to your intuition. Your life is no longer as constricted by the emotional pressures and intellectual preconceptions of your personality; instead, by a process of natural, spontaneous growth, you are developing an unfolding vision of yourself and others as components bound by implicate laws to the unified process that is reality.

From the transpersonal point of view, this is experienced as a great release from life's burdens; the burdens may still be there and have to be endured, but one's attitude to them has profoundly altered. Through a growing feeling of reconciliation and harmony with all that happens, one experiences the movement of responsibility for the direction of one's life to a force both within and outside the self. It is a feeling of free dependence, based on a calm acceptance of the harmony inherent in reality.

This free dependence on reality is your birthright. It is yours simply by committed daily practice of the meditation, coupled with sustained effort to understand your life in the context of these teachings. In this way, within a hundred days, it is possible to attain the first, or psychological, stage of enlightenment.

5 *Confirmatory experiences*

How is this chapter to be used?

This chapter can usefully be read by anyone. Unlike the remainder of the book, it is written exclusively from the transpersonal point of view. Accordingly, what is described in this chapter will only be fully realisable by those who have attained the first stage of enlightenment.

| | | | | | | | | |

Welcome, and congratulations. You have struggled long and hard, requiring all your courage and powers of endurance to overcome your fears and difficulties. Now is the time to rest and take stock of your new and growing awareness of reality.

You have successfully completed the first and most difficult step along the path to understanding the unity of reality through experience. Become aware of and enjoy your newfound freedom. By now, you know as a certainty that there are such things as enlightenment and a path, and that you are firmly set on that path.

Do not be proud of your achievement: instead, become aware of the wonder of reality as it unfolds to your inner vision. Learn not to be self-seeking in the face of reality: realise that it is not 'I' who lives, but 'that' which lives you. Care for others: as you travel along the path you will realise that we are all indissolubly linked in the face of reality; no-one in existence is exempt from karma.

You have struggled much, endured much, understood much. Yet, for all that, your work has only begun. You are now correctly positioned to understand, through your own experience, the nature and purpose of reality.

Remember, the way ahead is long and hard. In terms of emotional suffering the searing pains and tensions of the time of testing will grow dim as your capacity to operate free from intellectual and emotional constaints grows bright. Just as your present awareness completely transcends the limitations of what was your ordinary, everyday awareness, so, too, does the awareness brought about by the final stage of enlightenment transform and transcend your present limitations.

The worst is past, yet the hardest challenge lies ahead. This apparent contradiction is resolved by developing your latent abilities and powers; these will develop spontaneously to assist you as you travel along the path. All that counts, in reality, is where you are along the path in relation to the final stage of enlightenment: between the first and last stages of enlightenment are many transformations of consciousness, but all that matters at any one time is the next step along the path to the final stage of enlightenment.

What, then, is the final stage of enlightenment? The logical conclusion of this teaching of the clear setting face to face with reality must be that the final stage of enlightenment is to realise the unconditioned state; but it is not only for yourself that this is to be done. Full, absolute and final enlightenment is only realised when compassion for the unenlightened is awoken – regardless of the outer form of that life, the fully enlightened person is dedicated, through unremitting inner perseverance, to assisting all others to realise the unconditioned state.

The uses of this chapter are twofold. Firstly, practice of the meditation technique taught here will assist you to stabilise your new awareness, to settle firmly in the psychological stage of enlightenment. Secondly, continued practice in meditation, as directed, will prepare you for the full teaching contained in chapter 2 of the follow-up work from the Implicate Technology Centre, *The advanced guide to enlightenment*[1]. That chapter teaches how to integrate a life based on meditation into your social, moral, economic and political environment.

☆ ☆ ☆ ☆

---

[1] In preparation.

What are the differences between the first stage of enlightenment and an awareness based on a gradual integration into, and involvement with, your wider cultural environment?

The primary function of this book is to provide a simple self-help technology which, with committed daily use, leads to the first significant transformation in consciousness. The technology leading to the full understanding of reality through experience is beyond the scope of this book. The secondary function of this book is to enhance the implicate technology skills developed to attain the first stage of enlightenment, so that you will be able to set your life in harmony with the wider cultural forces shaping your environment: the moral, social, economic and political conditions.

To achieve this, one needs both a model of reality and an understanding of the true nature of meditation. The model of reality serves as a goal; only when the accuracy and completeness of the model is realised is the final stage of enlightenment attained. Meditation is the priceless, free tool available to each of us to assist us in the transforming and transcending of the conditions of our lives.

The model of reality is this: the true nature of reality is consciousness without content, which none the less permits all contents to exist. This cannot be understood within the range of experiences accessible to a person with a normal level of consciousness. A person who has attained the first stage of enlightenment is correctly positioned at the start of the path which leads towards understanding the fulness and unity of reality through experience.

The experience you are aiming for is to understand what is meant by a consciousness without content. To be able to experience this, you must develop your understanding through further committed daily practice of meditation. The true purpose of meditation is to develop your ability to still the process of thinking.

To still the thinking, to transcend the thought process, is a skill which you will develop, quite naturally and spontaneously, through meditation. As your everyday experience unfolds, you will gradually realise that your experience up to attaining the first stage of enlightenment has completely misled you as to the nature of reality. The goal of the culturally integrated and committed level of awareness, as discussed extensively in chapter 2 of *The advanced guide to enlightenment*, is to understand, with an intuitive certainty of knowledge, the true nature of reality; keep in mind, though, that this is not yet direct experience of the true nature of reality.

☆ ☆ ☆ ☆

What is the meditation on serenity and harmony?

There are many, many possible confirmatory experiences to be had after attaining the first stage of enlightenment, which may seem strange, simple, wonderful, even frightening. What you will experience will be a function of your own nature and individual gifts. Remember, everything you experience is karmically configured to lead you towards understanding your own nature.

To realise that a thing is so is to confirm it through experience. As this phase of the meditation unfolds, you will have many experiences which are real to you, but very difficult to articulate to others. The reason for this is that they are too simple to be expressed in words. Yet they are profoundly satisfying to experience.

To practice any of the meditations taught in this chapter you need to make one slight and difficult change in your daily meditation. Count the breaths and think only of the subject of your meditation; cut off all other trains of thought or fantasies. Remember, the goal is attained by living in meditation.

After the first stage of enlightenment, as your experience in meditation unfolds, the practice of counting the breaths may become an irrelevant distraction for you. Provided you are able to concentrate your thoughts on the subject of your meditation, there is no harm in gradually dropping the practice of counting breaths. The purpose of all meditative practices is to develop the ability to concentrate your attention on one thing at a time.

The aim of the meditation on serenity and harmony is to analyse your current condition. Become aware of your detachment, its benefits and how you arrive at this inner calm. Above all, learn how to sustain it for longer and longer periods.

The key to a full unfolding of your awareness, in the face of reality, lies in expanding your capacity to experience serenity and harmony in the midst of conditions. By attaining the first stage of enlightenment, you have broken free of the emotional and intellectual conditions constraining your personality. You will rapidly learn through experience that you have to work hard to sustain your new detachment – some days are warmer, some days are cooler.

Serenity is based on the capacity to remain detached from emotional conditions. You will still experience your own emotions and those of others; only, now, you need no longer be driven by these forces. Through serenity, you can transcend your habitual emotional behaviour patterns.

With practice at this meditation you will become increasingly free to choose your response to each set of conditions you experience. To operate in harmony, simply Live and Act throughout your life. Your karmic task is to benefit yourself and others through your actions.

Do not think that because you can sustain this state of serenity and harmony, you possess any inherent or acquired superiority over others. In reality, there is only one path for us all, and you are simply further along that path than others. You convey your understanding of these teachings primarily through your behaviour. Words are secondary to this.

☆ ☆ ☆ ☆

What is the meditation on the model of reality?

The root Implicate Technology image of reality is: consciousness without content, which none the less permits all contents to exist. The truth of this is all-embracing. The function of this meditation is limited to preparing your understanding only; the meditations leading to experience of the final stage of enlightenment will be included in the follow-up teaching from the Implicate Technology Centre on the nature and purpose of reality: *The advanced guide to enlightenment.*

The nature of your mind reflects the nature of reality: your mind is a microcosm of reality. The first stage of the process leading to a fully unfolded experience of reality is to develop an understanding of your mind. When you have understood the structure and functioning of your mind, you will then be in a position to experience the inherent unity and fulness of reality.

The function of meditation, when sustained with committed effort over time, is to produce a still mind. Put simply, this is the mind in its natural state, fully aware and freed from the tyranny of the thought process. You need give no thought at this stage to this process of developing a still mind; it will occur quite naturally as you develop your work in meditation, as taught in this chapter and chapter 2 of *The advanced guide to enlightenment.*

The mind, when uninhibited by the process of having thoughts, perceives clearly that the true experience of reality is of existence unfolding spontaneously, according to the inherent implicate laws. A measure of your progress towards advanced meditation is the development of the capacity to experience your life as unfolding naturally and spontaneously. Be clear: any thought or action, occurring outside of Act's guidelines, acts against the flow of reality and incurs negative karmic consequences, whose nature will be according to the true needs of your nature.

Through sustained, committed meditation, the thought-process slows gradually and imperceptibly. The richest fruits of meditation can only be realised once one understands, through experience, that the true nature of mind is emptiness and silence. A measure of your progress towards the advanced meditative practices is to be found in the relative decrease in the pace of the thoughts; when you experience thoughts as unfolding interminably and endlessly, but more slowly this week than last week, then you are progressing in meditation.

A mind which has attained emptiness and silence is far more aware and more powerful than a mind operating at the level of normal consciousness or the first stage of enlightenment. Such a mind is aware of its contents and is no longer preoccupied with compulsive satisfaction of needs and desires. The world, as rich and beautiful as ever in its fulness, still unfolds moment by moment, but it no longer dominates consciousness.

When the fulness of the world ceases to press on consciousness, then the mind turns naturally towards understanding the nature and purpose of reality. Before you can fully understand reality through experience, you must understand the nature of your own mind. You must first understand that the thoughts in your mind create your experience of reality.

From your own attainment of the psychological stage of enlightenment, you will be aware how the experience of emotional conditions is significantly determined by one's unconscious emotional projections. The emotions you were unaware of, before the first stage of enlightenment, none the less deeply shaped the experiences of your life. Changes in your feelings produced corresponding changes in your conception of the external world.

From your current, relatively enlightened, perspective, you now can understand that the emotional conditions experienced are relatively illusory, because they are the externalised products of mind. There is a general principle embodied here which is equally applicable to all conditions. Meditate on this long and hard; when you have developed an intuitive understanding of this principle, you will be clearly set on the path to advanced meditation.

☆ ☆ ☆ ☆

What is the meditation on the unity of time?

To ordinary consciousness, time is experienced as yesterday, today and tomorrow. Yesterday is the subject of individual memory and cultural history; tomorrow is the subject of individual and cultural fears and hopes. Ordinary consciousness is rarely located in today, here and now.

Our cultural habits reinforce and reflect this fragmented view, which is a product of the unenlightened mind. This individual and cultural fragmentation of time into the separate elements of past, present and future is real to the unenlightened, but relatively illusory to those who have attained the first stage of enlightenment. In reality, past, present and future function as a unified force.

The purpose of this meditation is to help you realise the unity of time. Practice in this meditation will develop your intuitive understanding of the unity of past, present and future in each set of circumstances you experience now. Understanding the true nature of time, through experience, is within the grasp of anyone who has broken free of the emotional and intellectual personality limitations; that is to say, one who has attained the first stage of enlightenment is in a position to understand that reality always, and only, unfolds now.

The illusion of the past being separate from the present is broken through realising that all of your past, increasingly distilled and refined in meaning as you progress along the path, is retained in your mind. The past is never settled in the relatively enlightened mind; its meaning and significance are continuously being understood in new and wider contexts, as awareness unfolds in the face of reality. Karma is the link incorporating the past into the present: what occurs now, spontaneously, is the karmic outcome of your previous choices.

The illusion of the future being separate from the present is broken through realising that the future, in its full potential, is inherent in seed form in the present moment. To the relatively enlightened mind, the future is beheld as unfolding from the potential of the present; its potential meaning and significance is continuously understood in new and wider contexts. Karma is the link incorporating the future into the present: what will occur, spontaneously, will be the outcome of present thoughts and actions.

The present, incorporating past and future, unfolds spontaneously and uncontrollably, according to the implicate laws inherent in conditioned existence. To the relatively enlightened person, awareness unfolds spontaneously, ever spiralling outwards in the face of reality. Each moment is understood and experienced simply and directly, on its own terms.

Meditate long and hard on the unity of time. Time is one of the key conditions you must understand, through experience, before you can attain the final stage of enlightenment. Once you have mastered this meditation you are in a position to understand the true nature of time: which is that you, your thoughts and all of conditioned existence, unfold, now, in the face of consciousness.

☆ ☆ ☆ ☆

What is the meditation on hearing?

Not all of the confirmatory experiences can be expressed in words; reality is too simple and unified for words. What you will experience is a function of your own nature and karma. If you accept these experiences as real, then they are real to you.

The purpose of these confirmatory experiences is to help you to understand the links between your own nature and reality. As you will gradually learn, the experiencing of reality solely through the five senses is limited and relatively illusory compared to the experiencing of the enlightened state. This meditation on hearing is an illustration of the general principle that reality is not structured, and does not function, in a way that is comprehensible within the limitations of sight, hearing, smell, taste and touch.

Reality only becomes comprehensible when one activates one's sixth sense of direct intuitive perception. Committed daily practice of meditation develops your sixth sense. As your intuitive perception of reality unfolds, you will experience a subtle, but real and lasting, change in your sense of hearing.

As the meditation takes holds and produces fruit, one's way of hearing alters, naturally and spontaneously. One becomes aware of hearing the ordinary sounds of the environment in a different way. One experiences sounds in this way: each is heard quite clearly, quite separately, and each is equally significant in your hearing.

Through meditation on this experience, one comes to realise how constrained is the hearing of normal consciousness. The lesson of this meditation is simple. Life is: become aware.

☆ ☆ ☆ ☆

What is the meditation on sexual energy?

To progress along the path to advanced meditation, to realise the meaning and purpose of existence requires a source of energy to power the final, massive transformation of consciousness. The teachings of this book, when fully realised, will guide you in your work with karma, and prepare you for the advanced meditations on the meaning and purpose of existence. This meditation, which requires much hard to work master, will prepare your whole being for the full experiencing of the unity of reality.

All models of reality take a stance on the role of sexuality in life. The Judeo-Christian tradition advocates confining sexual activity within a religiously sanctified, heterosexual marriage. Many religious models of reality advocate renouncing sexual activity altogether and re-channelling the sexual energy through chastity, via a life as a priest, nun or monk.

Most models of reality take a moral attitude towards sexual activity, allowing this and barring that. The Implicate Technology secular model of reality relies for its morality on the inherent moral patterning of existence, as imposed on all human beings by karma. Provided sexual activity is in harmony with the guidelines of Act, it matters not whether the activity is bisexual, homosexual or heterosexual, occurring inside or outside of marriage – all other constraints are not natural, being merely the products of moral, social, political and economic conditions.

From the secular point of view of Implicate Technology, all aspects of existence are understood as being, in practice, illusorily separate strands of an organically unified and purposive whole. In the face of reality, provided your sexual activity is in accordance with Act, your choice of partners and lifestyles is, simply, part of the raw material of your life, which you can refine through understanding into the experience of enlightenment. The primary issue, if you are to attain the final stage of enlightenment, through this or any other teaching, is not how conventional morality views your sexual orientation, but the correct use of your sexual energy.

It is not the purpose of this particular meditation to teach you the specific techniques of using the body's natural power source to attain the final stage of enlightenment. The scope of this meditation is confined to making you aware of the nature and functioning of your sexual energy, and to making a significant start on generating and utilising your body's implicate power source. The true nature and purpose of existence can only be realised through a form of implicate technology: sexual energy is the prime psycho-physiological link between your consciousness and the implicate nature of reality.

Be clear on this: your own sexual energy, stored within your body and properly used, in accordance with natural implicate laws, is the power source for the transformation of your consciousness. Through retaining, understanding and mastering your sexual energy, you attain full, final and absolute enlightenment. Through wasting your energy in unenlightened sexual activity, you will abuse the most precious gift your body produces for you.

The practice of this meditation is very simple to undertake, but very hard to sustain. It matters not if you fail, especially in the early stages – simply begin the meditation again. What is important is to develop an unwavering determination to succeed: temporary, even repeated, failure is less important than developing a singleness of mind to succeed.

The first step is to retain the sexual energy your body generates. If you are a man, this means retaining semen through avoiding ejaculation. If you are a woman, this means avoiding the release of sexual energy through clitoral orgasm.

Practice of this meditation does not preclude any form of sexual activity, provided it is in accord with Act. The meditation may also be practised during periods of celibacy or by renouncing sexual activity through chastity, provided such activities occur within the guidelines of Act. The key lies in retaining your sexual energy, not in the nature of your sexual activity.

Sexual activity involving this meditation can occur on your own through masturbation, or with a partner or partners. The practice in each case is the same: learn to refrain from physiologically-based orgasm. As you develop in this practice, through repeated failure then gradual success, you will begin to understand, slowly and naturally, the power inherent in your psycho-physiological system.

The practice of this meditation is the same for a person who does not experience orgasms. Your body's adaptive powers will compensate in a natural way. The essence of the technique lies in transmuting retained sexual energy.

The goal is not complete abstention from physiological orgasm. A fair but demanding target to set yourself is thirty days between orgasms. Be clear: this need not mean thirty days between sexual activities; that is a function of personal choice and the circumstances of your life.

Do not delude yourself that physiological orgasm is a great pleasure and release which you cannot do without. You only think this because you have nothing to compare such orgasms with. Be assured: the pleasures you will experience, on many levels of your being, will transcend, in intensity and power, anything unenlightened sexual activity can offer.

The actual techniques you use to refrain from physiological orgasm are a matter of personal experience and choice, subject to Act. There are many books offering sound advice for men on delaying ejaculation; there are very few for women on delaying clitoral orgasm. Our culture promotes achieving orgasm for both men and women: as you develop in this meditation, you will come to understand, through personal experience, that the key sexual activity is to practise retaining the sexual energy naturally and spontaneously produced by your body.

The key to realising this control is to understand, through meditation, that a physiologically-based orgasm is triggered by mental activity. As you learn to control your mind, you will learn to control your orgasms. All physically-based control techniques are inferior to this level of mental control.

The second step, in this yoga of sexual energy, is to understand through experience the energy which is retained in your body by the practice of not having physiological orgasm. After sexual activity which does not realease the body's natural energy through physiological orgasm, there remains considerable tension in your psycho-physiological system. This tension can express itself in a range of symptoms, from simple muscular tension to thoughts whirling endlessly round until you think your head will burst.

The goal of this stage of the meditation is to attain control of the retained sexual energy so as to integrate it into your whole psycho-physiological system, your whole, conditioned, being. You gain nothing by attempting to rush this process or by blaming yourself for failure. What you are trying to develop, above all else, is the unwavering determination to succeed in this meditation.

Your position at the beginning of the second step in this meditation is simple. You have engaged in sexual activity on one or more occasions, alone or accompanied, and through the habit of your body, or effort and practised determination, you have refrained from the release of physiological orgasm. Sooner or later, you will need or desire the release of orgasm to free you from the tensions sweeping your body and your mind.

It is this need or desire for the release of orgasm which you will now learn to transcend. Be patient and meditate long and hard. As you develop mastery, over a sustained period of committed practice, you will learn to experience pleasure in entirely new and satisfying ways.

The method of releasing yourself from the tensions sweeping your body and mind is twofold. Firstly, at any time, enter into the deep, slow breathing you have become accustomed to from your meditation practice. Secondly, learn to raise your retained energy from the sexual energy centre in your groin to the highest energy centre at the crown of your head.

Begin with a transition, willed or spontaneous, to deep, slow, meditative breathing. Do this during sexual activity, while working, while just relaxing at home or in any circumstances you can. The meditative breathing will help you to become centred in the midst of conditions.

This is a process you learn to achieve by experience. There are virtually no sets of conditions during which meditative breathing cannot be entered into. You must be your own teacher in this matter.

Now, with greater or lesser ease, you have settled into meditative breathing. Your psycho-physiological organism, your mind and body, is in a state of tension. You need or desire the release of orgasm.

The source of this disturbance in your whole organism is the sexual energy you have retained through not experiencing the pleasure and release of physiological orgasm. This energy, naturally produced every day by your body, and retained either by your body's natural functioning or by an act of experienced will, is located, at first, in the sexual energy centre. Your task now is to raise this energy to the crown energy centre: by first achieving, then sustaining, this practice, you generate all the power you will need to transform your experience of reality.

From your experience to this stage, you know, as a fact, that your body has a sexual energy centre located in your groin, and that your organism is keenly aware of the unrefined, hard to control, all-consuming nature of this energy. Now you are ready to begin the natural process of refining and transmuting this raw energy. You will learn either to raise this energy or to release it, usually via orgasm: for what seems the longest time, you will probably utilise both practices.

Before you begin the practice of raising and transmuting your body's naturally produced sexual energy, it will be helpful if you have some understanding of how your psycho-physiological organism is constructed to accommodate and assist this process. Be clear: you have no need to understand the mechanics of this process to achieve success in transmuting sexual energy. Your heart lasts a lifetime, whether you understand its functioning or not.

The sexual energy, raised, purified and transmuted naturally, flows round your body in a continuous circular motion, powered by each inhalation and exhalation of breath. With the in-breath, the energy rises from the sexual energy centre, physically moves up the spine to the back of the brain, then moves to the crown of the head. With the out-breath, the energy passes to the front of the brain, down through the tongue which is touching the roof of the mouth, and down through the chest, accumulating in a swirling motion in the abdomen before returning to the sexual centre.

This cyclic flow of energy occurs naturally and spontaneously as you develop in this meditation. In time, with diligent daily practice, the energy will flow entirely automatically, requiring no effort on your part. This is a very good sign: be satisfied with your progress, not pleased with yourself.

In the practices of the Taoist esoteric yoga, Tibetan Buddhist yoga and Hindu Kundalini yoga can be found very detailed and precise techniques to achieve this circulation of energy. These yogas are the product of very sophisticated, highly developed, implicate technologies. From the perspective of our Western cultures, based on the Judeo-Christian code of ethics and lacking broad-based spiritual depths, these yogas require specialised cultural terms which make them generally inaccessible to our spiritually under-developed Western societies.

This meditation, in fact this whole book, is an attempt to articulate the first steps in the process of integrating oneself fully into reality, in terms accessible to an ordinary, intelligent, Western person. What is taught here is a yoga as valid as its Eastern counterparts. It is expressed in a simple direct way because, spiritually speaking, we in the West are at a post-primitive and pre-civilised stage of cultural development.

Begin, then, the second step of the meditation on sexual energy. This involves a focussing of your awareness. This is simple to explain but hard for you to realise. Once you have gained the experience and skills to realise this step of the meditation, the natural functioning of your organism will spontaneously take over, and the energy will circulate, without any effort on your part, in a harmonious manner.

The practice required to raise the sexual energy, to power your own internal dynamic forces is simple. During the deep, slow in-breath, visualise the energy travelling from your groin, up your spine, to the very top, the crown, of your skull. During the deep, slow out-breath, visualise the energy travelling down from the crown, through the roof of your mouth, which your tongue is touching, down the front of the chest, through the abdomen, and back to the groin.

At the beginning of this practice the energy will most likely move in your imagination only. But as your skill devlops with unwavering determination, you will, in time, experience the actual movement of this energy. Be assured that this is fact, not theory or fantasy.

If it helps you in the early stages, focus your awareness on an image of erotic significance to you, and in your imagination visualise this image located at the crown of your head. This is an aid which should be discarded once you have learned to raise your sexual energy. To be successful in your quest for enlightenment, you must face reality directly, not through your fantasies.

Once the energy begins to circulate naturally, spontaneously and effortlessly, the tensions in your organism will begin to resolve themselves. Your power and understanding will grow, as the circulating energy is transmuted into a clearer and clearer understanding of the nature and purpose of reality. Without succeeding in this practice, you cannot attain the final stage of enlightenment: success is available to you, regardless of the conditions of your life, provided you Act and meditate with unwavering determination.

6 *The all-pervasive influence of the emotions*

What is the all-pervasive influence of the emotions?

Every situation you experience can be analysed and understood as a specific arrangement of the ten conditions. The goal of the process of enlightenment is to free you, progressively, from the constraints of the ten conditions. The first stage of enlightenment gives you the capacity to sustain freedom from emotional and intellectual limitations.

This teaching emphasises the crucial importance of breaking free from the emotional constraints of your personality. Until you do this, you cannot begin to see the world as it is. As long as you operate within the emotional conditions of your personality you will have a distorted view of reality.

Prior to the first stage of enlightenment, one seeks satisfaction of emotional needs and desires; afterwards, emotional satisfaction is not such a priority. Before the first enlightenment, one's view of the world is coloured by one's own attitudes; afterwards, you see that the emotional difficulties you experienced were primarily caused by your own emotions, by yourself and none other. Before the first stage of enlightenment, you are driven to attain emotional satisfaction and fulfilment; afterwards, you learn to deal with your life freely and spontaneously.

Through your emotional projections, a process you only gradually become aware of, you create the specific aspects of reality which you experience. The purpose of this period of your life is to test your capacity to recognise, and break free from, your unconscious emotional projections. These tests are karmic in nature, and are designed to establish the extent to which you are detached from your emotions, the extent to which you understand your own nature.

Remember, reality can be understood as a unified, organic machine, and each of us is an essential component. Part of the functioning of the process is a constant testing of your capacity to remain detached and clear. By becoming detached from your deep-seated emotional responses, you will attain the psychological stage of enlightenment.

☆ ☆ ☆ ☆

How does one experience karmic testing?

Throughout your life, you feel in turn joy and sorrow, and move up and down, endlessly up and down. In a vain effort to smooth out this process, some try to control others; some try to control themselves; and some try to endure the highs and lows. This constant experiencing of opposites, life's highs and lows, is a natural process; enlightenment offers the only real escape from this endless play of opposites in your life.

When you are far removed from the psychological stage of enlightenment, the alternation of joys and sorrows occurs as a long-term pattern flowing throughout your life. As you get closer to the first enlightenment, this alternating of joy and sorrow becomes more and more rapid. A person close to this stage of enlightenment experiences a profound lack of stability in both inner and outer emotional conditions.

It is important to distinguish between such emotional transformations leading to the unfolding of awareness, and the constant transformation in conditions experienced by the emotionally immature. The difference lies in developing your capacity to endure and persevere through time. One who is moving towards enlightenment understands the instability of conditions as a learning process; one who is emotionally immature simply desires to experience positive rather than negative emotional conditions.

The degree to which your emotions alternate between the opposites of joy and sorrow is a function of karma. The specific circumstances and conditions of your life are formed and structured, by karma, to test your capacity to become free from attachments to joys and sorrows. Learn to become responsive to the direction of karma in your life; trust in your karma to guide you through the maze of joys and sorrows.

The commonest response to the difficulties experienced during intense periods of karmic testing is: why me? The answer is: there is a lesson you have to learn before you can progress in your inner development, before you can progress along the path we each must travel, and your current situation is specifically configured, precisely drawn together, to enable you to understand and learn the lesson. Continue to meditate, Live and Act throughout your life, and the difficulties will be overcome.

Do not think, foolishly, that you can escape your karma. You cannot successfully swim against the flow of reality, because you are an integral component of the one reality. Remember, the implacable process that is reality will devour your personality and its products, at its own pace and in its own way – this is the root cause of your emotional suffering.

In the midst of your life conditions, blown here and there by karma, overwhelmed by difficulties and the illusion that they are permanent, your feelings may revolve around despair. Sustained despair can lead to the utterly false and illusory attempt to escape your problems through ending them by suicide. The only sure way out of the suffering experienced in all limiting emotional conditions is to cultivate detachment, yet to remain fully involved in your day-to-day life.

☆ ☆ ☆ ☆

How does one live a full emotional life, yet remain detached?

The detached attitude of mind which results from the successful application of these teachings is not to be confused with the male heterosexual insensitivity to emotional conditions which is such a common and inherently harmful product of our culture. Nor is it to be confused with that perversion of masculinity involving denial or suppression of emotions, either one's own or other people's. These forms of behaviour, which are by no means the sole province of the heterosexual male, are a failure to face reality and result in suffering caused by the accumulation of negative karma.

Be clear: after you have attained the first stage of enlightenment, you will still have the capacity to experience the full range of human emotions. What differs is that you will no longer be driven compulsively by your emotions. You will live and love both fully and freely, aware of the implications of the choices you make at each moment.

The heart of the matter is this: you must develop the ability to stand back from any situation you encounter through experience, to the extent that you understand your emotional response as being only one, relatively illusory, component of the conditions establishing that situation. In reality, the emotions experienced before the first stage of enlightenment are products of the personality and have only relative and illusory substance. After the psychological stage of enlightenment, you have the option to see through the illusion and to experience the emotions truly pervading all of reality.

To practise detachment, you need to resist the force of your emotions: use deep meditative breathing to calm you in emotionally stressful conditions. Learn to understand and experience difficult situations in a wider context which embraces both your point of view and the other person's. Learn to be detached: in reality, you may or may not get what you want in any particular situation – it truly does not matter. In either event, your life still goes on and the path unfolds, now, before you.

Use your meditation to develop your sensitivity to the full potential of each moment. Your emotional suffering is only real if you lack the capacity to detach yourself from it. Your emotional suffering will pass once you are centred in the midst of conditions.

☆ ☆ ☆ ☆

How does one become detached from fear and desire?

Fear and desire are deeply intertwined in our lives. What we desire most is often what we fear most. Fear is, in reality, the inverse of desire – "No! I don't want that."

Both fear and desire, experienced with intensity, can be very stressful on your whole organism, both mind and body. To become detached, you must free yourself from this stress, which invariably occurs on the path to the first enlightenment. The first and simplest technique is to enter into deep, slow meditative breathing – this will have a calming effect on your whole system.

There is also a second, more advanced, technique available to you. However, to develop in the practice of this second meditative skill you will require considerable faith. Not faith in anything particular, just faith.

Faith, pure and unbounded, grows in you naturally and spontaneously as your awareness unfolds of your role in the process that is reality. Your faith grows with the realisation of the fruits of meditation. Committed daily practice in meditation inevitably produces these fruits.

As the results of your meditation unfold, a simple fact will become clear to you. You will come to understand this fact gradually, with the certain knowledge of experience. This fact is that you and reality are one and indistinguishable.

This fact, which is the ultimate truth of reality, is not at all apparent to common sense. Only gradually will you come to understand what it means. When, finally, after many trials, you know through experience what it means, then and only then will you have attained the final stage of enlightenment.

Through time and meditation on your experiences, you will come to understand that you and karma are indistinguishably one. That is to say, everything that happens to you is a function of who you are and what you think, feel and do. It will slowly dawn on you that everything which happens in your life is part of a meaningful and purposeful pattern.

In time, with this realisation comes freedom from bondage to fear and desire. All along the path to the final stage of enlightenment, you will still have the capacity to experience fear and desire. However, through meditation, you can free yourself from attachment to fear and desire.

This freedom from attachment comes from realising that everything that happens in your life, everything, without exception, has meaning and purpose. All fear is relatively illusory, because what is happening, or will happen, is structured to teach you a lesson about your own nature. All desire is relatively illusory, because the conditions of your life will supply you with all you truly need to understand your own nature, which is the true nature of reality.

As your work in meditation develops, and your practical experience expands, you will experience a growing capacity for fearlessness and desirelessness in the face of reality. Reality is not to be feared, because you and reality are one. Trust what happens, however fearful, with a calm acceptance of the reality of life and death. Reality is not to be desired, because you and reality are one. Accept what you receive from life and have no doubt that it will be sufficient.

Put simply, whatever is happening will happen as it occurs; avoid letting your fear and desire interfere with the course of events. To develop your capacity for fearlessness and desirelessness, Live and Act throughout your life. Think long and deeply on this.

☆ ☆ ☆ ☆

Why is it crucially important to become detached from your anger?

Anger is the single most corrosive emotion you can experience. Anger stems from thwarted desire. Anger results from what you want being at odds with what you experience.

Anger is deceptively dangerous because it is such a satisfying emotion, particularly if, from one's own point of view, one appears to be in the right. Anger consumes your energies, and, if sustained over long periods, can consume your health. When you act in anger, it feels fulfilling, satisfying and righteous – in reality, it is an activity through which you oppose the natural flow of reality, and the resulting penalties which may be imposed on you can be horrendous.

To act on the basis of your anger is to insist on what you want, in the face of reality. This is the antithesis of the clear setting of yourself face to face with reality. You cannot successfully impose your will on reality without incurring severe penalties: sustained anger leads to sustained ill-health; profound anger leads, in time, to profound penalties.

As with all Implicate Technology disciplines, the remedy to be applied is simple. Firstly, when you are angry, calm yourself with deep, slow, meditative breathing. Secondly, never, ever, under any circumstances or conditions, act on the basis of your anger – wait until you are calm and then decide on your action.

This is not to say that you must passively accept the conditions that caused your anger. If the conditions you experience are unfair or unjust, use the power discipline, as taught in chapter 3, to change your circumstances. Fight, and fight hard, against forces which oppress you; but do so in harmony with the inherent implicate laws.

Don't act while you experience anger in the circumstances of your domestic life. Always wait until you have regained calm. If your anger is prompted by another person's genuine selfishness, the opportunity to act will invariably arise again.

The danger you risk is quite clear. If you act under the influence of anger, you will incur karmic consequences of a severely negative nature, according to the severity and duration of your anger. If you act spontaneously, with a calm clear mind, you will be dealing with any situation in a karmically positive way.

☆ ☆ ☆ ☆

Why is it crucially important to forgive?

In your life it can happen that you are wronged – unfairly, unjustly and apparently without rhyme or reason. Your sense of injury, in such a situation, is acute and very often considerably justified. If your pain is deep, and your sense of having been wronged is considerable, you may feel it is impossible, indeed stupid, to forgive one who has so clearly and unjustly mistreated you.

Be clear: when when such situations occur in your life, you are being tested by the process that is reality. The operator, structuring the situation to create your pain and sorrow, is the implacable law of karma. Whether you are able to forgive, or not, will significantly determine the shape of your life.

Christianity teaches the moral necessity for forgiveness. The supreme example of forgiveness, in our Western cultures, is set by Jesus accepting and forgiving the suffering of his crucifixion, so that the prophecies of his culture might be fulfilled, and primitive peoples raised to an ethically-based civilisation. The secular Implicate Technology teaching of the clear setting face to face with reality deals only with the mechanics of the process of forgiveness – the morality of each situation is dealt with by your responding positively to the promptings of your karma.

The mechanics of the process of forgiveness are simple. If you remain attached to your suffering, and are unable to forgive, you will continue to incur negative karma. If you forgive the person or persons who wronged you, you will be relieved from the weight and burden of your accumulated negative karma, according to the degree of your forgiveness.

If you refuse to forgive the wrongs done to you, you will remain bound to the pattern of pain and sorrow which has brought about such a significant opportunity in your life. If you refuse to forgive, you are reinforcing your commitment to unenlightened behaviour. Reality will so structure itself that the opportunities to forgive will continue until you learn the lesson – this means you will continue to suffer through the workings of your karma.

To commit an act of genuine forgiveness is to release yourself from bondage to a specific pattern of pain and sorrow in your life. To forgive is to confirm your commitment to enlightenment, to affirm your determination to act in accordance with the flow of reality. Now reality will so structure itself, because you have learnt an important lesson, that your life moves on to the next lesson. This does not mean the end of your pain and sorrow; it simply means an opportunity to move closer to enlightenment.

The act of forgiveness is simplicity itself. Words alone are not forgiveness. Reality is beyond mere words such as: "I forgive you".

For the forgiveness to be a genuine release from the burden of accumulated negative karma, it must involve a sincere stepping away from attachment to your pain and sorrow. Mere words may fool other people; they can never fool karma. Within yourself, you must become committed to detachment from your suffering – only then does the genuine act of forgiveness take place.

The first step in the sincere act of forgiveness is to become detached from your negative emotional responses. Calm, slow, meditative breathing will help you to achieve this. Think about this teaching in the context of your own life, long and carefully.

The second step in the sincere act of forgiveness is to convey the fact that you have forgiven to the person or persons who have wronged you. This can be conveyed in simple words, when and if a suitable opportunity arises. What you have to say, according to circumstances, is some variation on this theme: "These things happen. I was hurt, but we can all learn from experience".

Do not, foolishly, believe that a genuine act of forgiveness will cause your pain to disappear rapidly, nor that your life will suddenly be filled with what you desire as a reward. The consequence of a sincere act of forgiveness is to release you from the burden of your accumulated negative karma. The true benefit you derive, freed from attachment to your pain and sorrow, is to be set clearly face to face with your experience of reality. In this way, you progress along the path to enlightenment.

☆ ☆ ☆ ☆

What is the Implicate Technology teaching on the act of unconditioned giving?

A true act of giving is a gift from yourself to another, devoid of ulterior motive. A gift which is given with the expectation of a specific response is a limited, conditioned gift. True giving requires no particular response and is meaningful and beneficial for you whether or not the gift is accepted by the recipient.

The attitude of mind in which you give is of crucial importance. The true act of giving involves a natural, spontaneous desire to enhance the life of the recipient. Give according to your own intuitive nature, without being influenced by thoughts of the consequences for yourself.

Give without any strings attached. An act of giving with an expectation of certain responses is only manipulation of others disguised as generosity. Such an act produces negative karma.

True giving is an act carried out purely for the sake of the recipient. Once the gift is truly given you retain no hold or rights over it. The positive or negative karmic consequences of your action will be determined by the interaction between yourself and the recipient.

The teachings contained in this book are given freely to you, with no conditions attached. Teachings which lead to enlightenment are beyond price, so only the insignificant cost of this book is involved. This gift, the teaching of the clear setting face to face with reality, the practice leading to the clear understanding of the meaning and purpose of your life, is offered to you to enrich your life.

What is given to you through this teaching is given freely. You are free to make of this gift whatever you are able to. You owe nothing to the Implicate Technology Centre for this gift.

A gift can be repaid in many, many ways. True giving requires no material recompense. The gift of these teachings is repaid in full, as your life is enriched and transformed through the practice of these teachings.

7 *Advice on failure to attain the psychological stage of enlightenment*

There is no lasting or necessary reason why you should not attain the release, freedom and fulfilment characteristic of the first stage of enlightenment. It is an experience well within the grasp of any ordinary, intelligent person who is prepared to live fully and honestly. This chapter reviews various causes for apparent failure and provides guidance to set you back on the path.

☆ ☆ ☆ ☆

In terms of your own life, how do you measure the success or failure of this teaching?

Any statement about reality, if it is to be of general relevance and usefulness, must be subject to a simple practical test to establish its validity. If any individual or group makes an observation on an aspect of reality which is not susceptible to a simple test to establish its validity, then either the observation needs refining until such a test can be found, or the observation is irrelevant in the face of reality. This teaching of the clear setting face to face with reality must satisfy such a simple, practical test to establish its validity.

You can only establish the value and accuracy of the description of reality contained in this book through your own experience. Your intellectual views and personal beliefs are irrelevant distractions in the face of reality. Just as you are subject to the law of gravity, regardless of whether you think about it or approve of it, so you are subject, in the same way, to the implacable implicate laws of reality, regardless of whether you accept these teachings or not.

You are set on the path to experience reality fully only after you have attained the first stage of enlightenment. Then, as your confusion and uncertainty about the meaning and direction of your life diminishes, you will be able to confirm the validity of this teaching through your own experience. You can use a simple test of the validity of this teaching to provide you with a measurable goal during the period of uncertainty and confusion about your life.

This test, to be applied by you in the course of living your life, is simple and straightforward. The key to the validity of this whole teaching is attaining the first stage of enlightenment. The test is this: after one hundred days of committed daily practice of meditation, understood within the context taught in this book, have you attained the psychological stage of enlightenment?

If the answer is yes, then you will know with the certainty of experience that there are indeed two such things as enlightenment and a path. If the answer is no, then you need to establish whether the failing lies in yourself or in the teachings. Committed practice of the teachings given in this chapter should set you back on the path to the first enlightenment; if that fails to help you, then you must draw your own conclusions about the validity and relevance of this teaching for you.

☆ ☆ ☆ ☆

'For one hundred days I have practised meditation with full commitment, yet I don't feel enlightened – why not?'

There are many reasons why this may be your experience. None of them are lasting or very important. The key activity is to continue committed daily practice of the meditation.

If you have genuinely meditated, for a minimum of fifteen minutes daily, for one hundred consecutive days, you will undoubtedly have experienced considerable benefit. You will feel more aware of your strengths and weaknesses, more in touch with the centre of your life and more able to deal with the daily pressures and problems of your life. Your life is enriched but still you do not feel enlightened.

One hundred days is only a guideline, nothing more. A healthy person, fully committed, can attain the first stage of enlightenment in well under one hundred days; a sick person may require longer to develop the whole organism's natural capacity for enlightenment. What counts above all is the intensity of effort and the degree of seriousness with which you apply yourself to the meditation and the teachings.

It may be that, although you have enriched your life, you have given up any hope of enlightenment for yourself. You have contented yourself with the knowledge that enlightenment can be attained by ordinary, intelligent people. However, for some reason not at all clear to you, your karma seems to be that you will not attain what is accessible to others more fortunate than yourself.

This is a natural feeling and a very good sign. Maintain or even increase your efforts and put all thoughts of enlightenment out of your mind. Focus your thoughts on the meditation and its effects on your life.

The Implicate Technology path to enlightenment entails a gentle, gradual and wholly natural progression along the path of understanding through experience. There is no sudden burst of enlightenment with this method. Simply, one day soon, you will look back and realise that you have been psychologically enlightened for a week or two.

☆ ☆ ☆ ☆

'I have practised the meditation intermittently, with no sustained effort, and it seems to produce no worthwhile results – why not?'

Your whole organism, your mind and body, in reality linked inextricably as a unity, is structured with the built-in desire, capacity and ability to attain enlightenment. The drive to attain enlightenment is a natural part of your existence – the aim of meditation is to awaken and fulfil that drive. The capacity to become psychologically enlightened is well within the ability of any ordinary intelligent person.

The purpose of the simple meditation technique taught in this book is to awaken, strengthen, mature and bring to successful fruition your in-built capacity for attaining enlightenment. The way to achieve this is committed daily practice of meditation. It is only with sustained duration of effort through time that your inherent capacity to attain enlightenment will awaken.

The reason you have achieved so little is because you have committed so little of your self. Out of arrogance, laziness or fear, you have only dipped a toe in the water, or only rolled your trousers up and gone paddling in the shallows. Then you wonder what there is in swimming which is so satisfying to other people.

Be clear on this: until you have sustained the practice of meditation through a period of time, you have not begun to meditate. Intermittent attempts to meditate are only intermittent attempts, nothing more. Unless you persevere with a minimum of fifteen minutes meditation daily, you will continue to live your self-illusory, self-deceiving and self-wasteful life.

By now, having tried meditation a little, you are probably aware of how demanding such a simple practice actually is. This is because living your life fully and honestly is very demanding. Think on this and what it tells you about yourself.

☆ ☆ ☆ ☆

'I am unconvinced that this book is anything more than words – how do I know if it is genuine or not?'

The answer to this question will be developed by use of a simple analogy. A child comes up to you and holds out a bag of sweets. The child asks you a simple question: how do you like the taste of the sweets?

The child, in this analogy, is this Implicate Technology teaching of the clear setting face to face with reality. The sweets offered are the fruits of meditation. The real question is: are these fruits genuine and attainable by you?

You could look at the wrapping on the sweets to see if the flavour is similar to something you have tried before. Equally, you could compare this book for similarities with any other books you may have read on meditation. In both cases, the response is intellectual only and fails to deal with the issue: how do you like the taste of the sweets?

You might be suspicious that the child is somehow trying to trick you, for a joke perhaps, and that the sweets are very bitter. You might be suspicious that this book is a hoax, and that the Implicate Technology Centre is trying to ensnare you in some elaborate trick. In each case you might be right – life can be full of nasty surprises. But how are you going to know for sure, and what might you miss if the offer is genuine?

You could ask the child if the sweets taste nice, just as you could find someone who has practised this or other meditation techniques and ask such a person about his or her own experience. How would that help you decide if you like the taste of the sweets?

You could take a principled stance and protest that sweets are bad for the teeth. You could stand on whatever principles you judge are relevant and say that meditation is not the sort of thing you believe in or approve of. You are only being asked to taste a sweet; you are only being asked, as a minimum commitment over a limited number of days, to sit down, look at the bridge of your nose and count your breathing. What are you afraid of?

You could react with a greater or lesser degree of emotional or intellectual aversion to either simple offer. If you are honest, such a response should make you question yourself. Why such a reaction to a very simple offer, with no strings attached?

There is, of course, only one way to find out if you like the taste of the sweets. There is only one way to find out if the fruits of meditation are genuine and attainable by you. Try it for yourself and observe what happens.

☆ ☆ ☆ ☆

'I have worked hard at meditation, made some progress, then I became stuck at some point – what is happening?'

There is one simple test to establish whether you are genuinely progressing towards enlightenment. The test is whether you experience your day-to-day life, in all its ordinariness, as a constantly unfolding process of change. If you experience your life as an endlessly flowing and changing process, then you are progressing along the path; if you experience your life as repetitive or static in its ordinariness, then you are stuck and will need to take corrective action before you can proceed along the path.

The teaching in this section identifies the most common faults which may block your progress on the path. It will provide you with practical advice on how to recognise and overcome the blocks. These blocks are purely temporary and can be overcome with the awakening of self-knowledge.

The whole process of enlightenment is to awaken your

self-knowledge. It is a considerable error to confuse self-knowledge with solely contemplating your personality. That is a very limited and destructive form of self-obsession, which has only the remotest connection with self-knowledge and the quest for enlightenment.

Attaining self-knowledge requires facing up to, and going beyond, the limitations of your personality. This is invariably a painful and unpleasant experience. It is also unavoidable if you are to attain enlightenment.

The basic error you are making, in your search for enlightenment, is that you are not facing up to the simple truths about yourself which reality is teaching you through the events of your life. This error occurs in two common forms in your life – failure to face those aspects of reality of which you are aware, and failure to face those aspects of reality of which you are unaware. Both incur severe karmic penalties, which you experience as emotional and physical suffering and misery.

You cannot escape from this apparently remorseless process of misery by attaining, or hoping to attain, some object you desire. As you progress along the path, you will discover that even desiring enlightenment is a block to attaining that state of freedom from emotional constraints. To pin your hopes of fulfilment and freedom on achieving this aim, or attaining that object or person, is to delude yourself with fantasy.

There is only one path to a genuine and lasting sense of joyous freedom and release from the misery of emotional and physical distress. That path is to set yourself directly face to face with reality as you experience it each moment. To be set on your journey along that path, you must learn to overcome the obstacles in your way.

☆ ☆ ☆ ☆

'How am I to recognise and deal with my own failure to face up to reality?'

Begin with an evaluation of your life as it is now. Lay aside all thoughts of whom you do, or do not, hold to be responsible for your current situation. In your quest for enlightenment, it will not help you, now or at any other time, to apportion blame for your conditions to yourself or to others.

As you proceed with this self-evaluation, there is one preliminary activity which it is essential to undertake if you are to be successful.

Learn to lay aside the bluff you have been running, the pretence you maintain to fool yourself and others that you understand and are in control of your life. Unless you conduct this evaluation honestly, you will fail and continue to incur the miserable consequences of negative karma.

The first and easier stage of this process of self-evaluation is to identify those areas of your personality in which you are aware that you refuse to face reality. The test to establish which are these areas in your personality is simple. Your usual response when an issue arises in such an area of your life is some variation on: 'I don't want to deal with this'.

Perhaps you find the aspect of life you don't want to deal with frightening or unpleasant. This may well be a genuine and valid reaction; nonetheless, unless you face up to the reality of your life, you will continue to incur the karmically imposed penalty of recurring misery. To proceed along the path to enlightenment, you must find the strength, the determination and the resolve to deal effectively with all that occurs in your life.

The way to harness your innate determination, to gather together your energies with a firm resolve, is to be found by including the insights resulting from your self-evaluation into your practice of meditation. During your daily meditation, whenever your thoughts shift from counting the breaths, focus your thoughts on the aspect of your life that you would prefer not to have to deal with. With practice of this simple discipline, in time you will find that a new perspective on the problem emerges: you will see your difficulties in a wider context, where they will become understood as less important to you.

The second and more difficult stage of this process of self-evaluation is to identify those areas of your personality in which you are unaware that you refuse to face up to reality. The test to assist you in establishing the necessary intuitive insights into your own nature is simple. All Implicate Technology tests are simple, and all require considerable clarity of thinking and self-honesty if they are to be applied successfully.

The test is this: to become aware of an important aspect of your life, although at present you are unaware of this part of yourself. To a greater or lesser degree, we all, without exception, suffer from this failing. Unless you succeed in this test, you will remain blocked, with all the dissatisfaction and unhappiness which that entails.

You cannot become conscious of something about yourself of which you are presently unconscious by observing the problem directly. What you can observe in your life directly, you are not unaware of. Instead, make a start by becoming aware not of the problem itself, the obstacle in your life preventing progress along the path to enlightenment, but of the effects on your life of the problem within yourself.

To progress in your self-knowledge, to satisfy the test so that you can proceed along the path to enlightenment, you need to become aware of the recurrent patterns in your life. That is to say, you are trying to find, by thinking back over your life, a series of events or emotions which crop up as disturbing repetitions in the events of your life. This process of self-analysis may encompass feelings of rejection, failure, bitter quarrels, deep frustrations or disappointments – the list of possibilities is endless.

Be clear: the sole cause of any recurrent patterns in your life is the interaction between your own nature and the workings of karma. This implacable implicate law of reality spontaneously structures the events of your life so as to bring to your attention the next aspect of your nature which it is necessary for you to understand if you are to progress along the path to enlightenment. Always keep this in mind: once you have become aware of a previously unknown limitation in your own nature, you have the opportunity to correct it and so make progress towards ending your unhappiness.

You can proceed with the test by working on yourself during your daily meditation. Do this by focusing your thoughts on the broad sweep of your life; through meditation, learn to understand the general trends of your life. After a time, and with sustained committed practice, your natural intuitive abilities will bring into your mind an awareness of the relevant pattern in your life.

When this happens, switch to the meditation practice taught in the first stage of this self-evaluation process. Now, when your thoughts drift from observing your breathing, focus them on the pattern in your life you have become aware of. Committed daily practice of meditation, incorporating the insights which spring from it into your daily life, is the key to breaking out of the pattern of misery and unhappiness at the heart of your life.

8 *Conclusion - the far journey*

What is the far journey?

To attain the goal of existence, to understand and experience the meaning and purpose of life, we each must travel the far journey. This is a journey within yourself to the realisation that 'you' and 'I', these teachings and all else are, in the final experience of reality, one and indistinguishable. The goal is the same for each of us, no matter whether expressed in religious or secular terms.

As you travel along the difficult path towards the final goal of freedom from the constraints of conditioned existence, you will need guidance and support. If you are to avoid the many traps, delusions and dead-ends which lie along the way, you will need to work within a soundly structured and fully developed model of reality. All the variations of self-delusion can be avoided if the model of reality you are working with has a detailed structure embracing the various stages of awareness and appropriate meditative practices to help you develop at each stage.

In reality, it does not matter which model you choose, whether this secular path or one of many religious paths according to your taste. What counts is the accuracy and thoroughness of the model and your commitment to its practices. When your daily activities form a living experession of the relevance of the model you are working in, then you will be progressing on the far journey.

☆ ☆ ☆ ☆

As you travel on this long inward journey to a complete realisation of the inherent unity of all that exists, how are you to relate to others in your life?

The area of personal relationships is fraught with difficulty. It is the primary set of conditions through which karma tests the extent of your detachment from your own needs and desires. Pursuit of this secular spiritual path of Implicate Technology does not absolve you of responsibility for the general and specific welfare of others.

How this responsibility is interpreted is a matter of great cultural and personal significance. The spiritual life is passionately demanding, all-absorbing and all-fulfilling; yet your achievements along the path will have only limited value if they serve to benefit yourself alone. One of the central issues you will have to face, on this secular path, is how to adapt your awakening spiritual perception, through sustaining the practice of meditation, to the needs and demands others will make on your life.

The great and ancient Eastern civilisations have developed solutions to this problem appropriate to the needs and forms of expression of their cultures. They have understood the necessity for complete absorption in the inner process of spiritual development, and have articulated culturally relevant, that is to say generally acceptable, ways of aiding this process. In general, the solutions of the Eastern civilisations have involved an act of renunciation of the typical everyday concerns of home, family and earning a living.

This act of renunciation in order to follow a spiritual path is supported by an ancient Eastern tradition of supplying food daily to monks begging in the streets. The ordinary person, according to the values of the Eastern cultures, earns merit by assisting the beggar following a spiritual path, by providing such people with daily food. In this simple way the general culture acts to support those dedicated to the spiritual path.

This act of renouncing family and friends, as well as material comforts, in pursuit of enlightenment is understood in the East as a positive act and not, as it seems to our Western scale of values, as a flight from responsibility. The Eastern paths to enlightenment usually involve single-minded dedication to the spiritual life alone. A spiritually dedicated person is understood, in a generally accepted sense, as contributing significantly to the quality of life in the Eastern cultures.

In our late-twentieth-century materialistic Western cultures, the situation faced by a person who aspires to the spiritual life is virtually the opposite of that found in the Eastern traditions. There are no generally acceptable cultural roles available for such people. In fact, in our Western societies, there is no widespread understanding of the spiritual path, either from a religious or a secular point of view.

In the face of this general and deep-rooted ignorance of the spiritual truths of life, the life of one who seeks to understand and experience the spiritual nature of reality can be beset with difficulties. The risk of incomprehension from friends, colleagues and loved ones is high. We in the West need to develop an entirely different approach from that worked out over millennia in the East to the issue of how to live a fulfilling and spiritually satisfying life.

The key to the Eastern approach is renunciation and separation: forsake home, family, friends and material comforts and mark yourself out by clothes and way of living as committed to a spiritual path. The key to this Western, secular Implicate Technology teaching is embracing and non-separation: absorb yourself in the needs of home, family, friends and wider social concerns and, in the day-to-day pressures of your life, learn to follow a spiritual path by living your ordinary life. The remainder of this chapter provides guidelines on how to mingle with the world and yet live in harmony with the inherent implicate laws governing our lives.

☆ ☆ ☆ ☆

What are the Implicate Technology guidelines for relationships with others?

The most rewarding and most difficult relationships are with those who share your life – lovers, friends, spouses, parents, children and those with whom you work and play. This Implicate Technology teaching of embracing the events of everyday life will assist you spiritually through the natural, flowing development and unfolding of the relationships in your life. The primary element linking your relationships with your spiritual development is continued daily practice of meditation – do this with commitment and your life will evolve with a natural spontaneity to take you along the path.

You will discover, as your practice in meditation develops, that the context in which you understand your experience as it spontaneously unfolds is all-important. The stress and difficulties of relationships can easily deflect you from the path of inner development and into the maze of emotional dead-ends which is the primary subject area of many of our psychologies. To safeguard yourself from these pitfalls, be aware of the constant presence of karma in the patterning of the everyday events of your life.

Be clear on this: every aspect of your life, from the major events to the tiniest details, is structured by the implicate law of karma to provide you with an environment in which you can best learn about your own nature. The relationships in which you find yourself involved are an intergral part of the karmic patterning of your life. You and those with whom you become involved are elements in a process inherently structured to enhance self-knowledge.

It is within this context that your relationships occur. When you experience stress or difficulty in personal matters, have compassion for any others involved. They too are undergoing the same slow and painful process of karmic conditioning.

As you apply yourself to the challenge of meditation and spiritual self-development, possibilities for change will unfold in your personal involvements with others. It may not be easy to introduce new attitudes and insights into established relationships. Have compassion and understanding for the difficulties others may have in adapting to the changes within yourself.

Our materialistic, outward-looking, late-twentieth-century, secular culture does little to prepare us for the complexities, difficulties and ambiguities of the process of inner change. The transformations in attitude and understanding involved can create fear in one who is unprepared for them. The conditions of your life, no matter how apparently difficult, are suffused with compassion – try to understand how this compassion operates, for the benefit of both yourself and others.

As you become absorbed in the emotional conditions shaping your life, try to maintain an attitude of detached compassion for yourself and others. Despite all difficulties, maintain your practice of meditation. Familiarise yourself with the techniques discussed in chapter 6 for the day-to-day handling of your emotions.

Allow yourself to understand that the fear and obstruction you may experience, as others react to the changes in you, is a function of our culture's ignorance of the process of inner transformation. You and those involved with you are engaged in a process of profound and joyous change. The responsibility lies with you to explain patiently what is happening, and to assist others in overcoming their fears and doubts.

☆ ☆ ☆ ☆

What are the Implicate Technology guidelines for using the abilities which will arise in you through the practice of meditation?

You will find yourself developing new abilities as you advance in your daily practice of meditation, particularly as you progress beyond the first stage of enlightenment. The follow-up work from the Implicate Technology Centre, *The advanced guide to enlightenment,* will discuss these abilities in a context which helps you to recognise the form and purpose of such experiences. The purpose of this section is to provide you with guidelines which will prepare you to use your abilities as they develop.

Throughout this book, you have been taught that the context within which you understand your experience of life is of prime importance. You will have given yourself totally to this Implicate Technology teaching of the clear setting face to face with reality if, throughout your life, you Live and Act. The context of this secular teaching encourages you to develop towards the final stage of enlightenment, the attainment of the unconditioned state, through the gradual realisation of your role in the culture you find yourself in.

In contrast with most Eastern paths to enlightenment, this Western secular path teaches you to absorb yourself in your immediate environment, both in the narrow personal and the wider cultural sense. The skills learnt from Implicate Technology disciplines direct you towards the final stage of enlightenment, through the understanding of the forces shaping your environment, and through integrating yourself with these forces. To achieve this, it is important to have a wide-ranging understanding of the stage of development at which our late-twentieth-century Western cultures have arrived.

We live in a culture which has been shaped by two thousand years of the Judeo-Christian code of ethics. That is to say, the standard by which it is culturally acceptable to us to judge behaviour is a code of values based on the Bible. Not everyone agrees with or adopts this standard of ethical behaviour, but the Bible has had an undoubted and marked influence on the development of Western ethical values.

Cultures go through phases of growth, maturity and decay, just like anything else. Occasionally it happens that cultures experience a qualitative upwards step, a quantum leap in development. Just as individuals can take unexpected leaps in their level of consciousness on the path to the final enlightenment, so too can whole cultures take evolutionary leaps.

In the late twentieth century, we in the West are living during a time of great cultural change. This is a period drained of the stability rooted in a firm belief in the Judeo-Christian code of ethics. At the same time, it is a period of immense potential – we are poised to take a leap from an ethically-based, to a spiritually-based, culture.

In the vanguard of this change will be those who have been enriched, in their own lives, by the natural progression towards the final stage of enlightenment. The first, or psychological, stage of enlightenment is accessible to any ordinary intelligent person through a hundred days of committed daily practice of meditation. As the number of people who understand the process of attaining enlightenment, and who become committed to their own progress along the path grows, they will come together, spontaneously, to create change for the good of all, according to the inherent implicate laws of reality.

For a person experiencing the path to enlightenment in our complex, stressful, ethically-based and spiritually-underdeveloped Western culture, the natural and instinctive goal is to seek out a role which allows the expression of one's inherent healing abilities. Your latent abilities will awaken, as you progress in your meditation. Expect nothing, have no preconceptions and be open to accepting your experience. Be clear: you are free to use the abilities developed through the practice of meditation for either selfish or unselfish ends; but you are not free to dictate the karmic consequences of your thoughts or actions.

To choose the path of unselfishness is to continue developing towards the final stage of enlightenment. To use the fruits of meditation for selfish, self-serving ends is to deviate from the path and simultaneously to incur karmic consequences designed to alert you to the error of your way. As you choose, so your life will unfold for you to experience. Nothing in your life, whether you are on the path or not, is a product of meaningless chance.

Committed daily practice of meditation will awaken your inherent ability to heal others and to enhance and enrich their lives. The form which this takes is a function of the activity of karma, which develops the component parts of the process of reality so that, individually and collectively, the component consciousnesses move through time towards an understanding of their unified nature. The underlying form of all meditation-enhanced healing is an inherent impulse to assist others to move towards enlightenment.

As your healing skills unfold, you will be spontaneously drawn to those who will both benefit from your skills and assist you to progress along the path. This Implicate Tehnology teaching of reaching enlightenment through embracing the events of everyday life results in mutual enhancement through a realisation of mutual dependency. When you benefit or harm another person or thing, you inescapably incur appropriate positive or negative karmic consequences, according to the true nature of your action.

The actual Implicate Technology guidelines for integrating yourself into the process of developing your cultural environment are straightforward, simple and very demanding:

1) Committed daily practice of meditation will develop your intuitive abilities (see chapter 2).

2) Become centred in the midst of conditions (see chapter 3).

3) Analyse the conditions of your life, in terms both of your developing abilities and the needs of those around you (see chapter 3).

4) Become sensitive to the direction in which karma is guiding your life (see chapter 4).

5) Act.

☆ ☆ ☆ ☆

What are the Implicate Technology guidelines for operating openly and yet unnoticed, for being different and yet the same?

There are no culturally approved, readily accessible roles available for an enlightened, or relatively enlightened, person in our late-twentieth-century Western cultures. We have no true cultural equivalent of the Eastern guru – a person who is recognised and accepted as having realised through inner experience the true nature of reality, and so has become fit to teach others how to attain this ultimate experience. Accordingly, those who follow the path begun in this book and to be completed in its successor, *The advanced guide to enlightenment*, will face the challenges, opportunities and dangers common to all pioneers.

You may have to deal with the incomprehension and hostility of those around you, as you seek to express your new-found understanding. The way to avoid conflict is to blend in with your environment. The way to change and enhance your environment is to lead by unspoken example.

This activity of leading, yet not being seen to lead, is achieved through the use of a by-product of your daily practice of meditation. Progress in meditation assists you to leave behind narrow, subjective, personal ways of behaving and experiencing reality. Learn to Act impersonally, without subjective regard for self or others.

The way ahead for our Western cultures lies not with those who merely talk about the nature of reality and enlightenment. The pressure to lift our understanding from an ethical to a spiritual base will be generated by those who show by their behaviour that they understand from their own experience. Integrate your enlightened understanding into your everyday activities and you will lead by example and influence others without being seen to do so. You will be different and yet the same.

☆ ☆ ☆ ☆

What is the goal of this Implicate Technology teaching of the clear setting face to face with reality?

The goal of this teaching is the same as that offered by any fully developed model of reality. This goal is to teach you to experience the final and absolute truth about the nature of reality. This Implicate Technology teaching is simply a path to the eternal truth, couched in language and concepts appropriate to late-twentieth-century Western secular culture.

The ultimate truth is so simple. It is nothing more than being in the unconditioned state. Dedicated, intelligent practice of these Implicate Technology teachings will lead you to that state of being.

Once the unconditioned state is realised, all becomes simple and clear. Where it is necessary to know, knowledge is effortlessly acquired; when it is necessary to act, action is effortlessly achieved. In that state, there is no divisive individuality and no conflict – there is only clarity, wisdom and delight in what is.

All this can only be fully understood once the final stage of enlightenment has been realised through experience. This book, followed with dedication and a fully committed intelligence, will lead you a little way beyond the first stage of enlightenment. This preliminary teaching, followed carefully in the light of your experience, will take you a little way into the state of mind beyond the personality.

The follow-up book being prepared by the Implicate Technology Centre, *The advanced guide to enlightenment*, will provide a teaching which enables one who has experienced the first or psychological stage of enlightenment to advance to the final and absolute goal. That book will provide detailed practical guidance on how to develop the necessary skills and mental states. It will also provide a rounded and clear model of reality, describing the nature and purpose of conditioned existence.

The ultimate goal, realisation of the unconditioned state, is an experience impossible to convey in words. Any given path to attaining that pure and original state of mind can only express understandings and insights from one particular cultural point of view. The one incommunicable truth, knowable only by direct experience, can be expressed through many different models of reality.

To be guided in your practice of these teachings, be mindful that the goal is simple. It can be conveyed in these few words: learn to live in meditation. The meaning of this is all-embracing.

The practice of meditation, properly directed, is to develop a mind capable of understanding through experience the true nature of reality. This is achieved by extending the understanding gained by the sustained practice of meditation to embrace every aspect of your life. The culmination of the meditative process lies in the development of a mind capable of experiencing all it witnesses as illusorily separate aspects of an inherently unified whole.

There is no sense of individual separation in such a state of being. Loneliness, pain and all joys and sorrows fade in significance before unconditioned mind. All things remain but, when set face to face with the clarity, wisdom and delight in what is, which are the hallmarks of the unconditioned mind observing conditioned existence, they are experienced as the relative illusion which they truly are.

☆ ☆ ☆ ☆

Religions, in common with Implicate Technology, offer a path leading to the full understanding of reality. Our Western religions require belief, worship and faith in God; this secular Implicate Technology teaching requires practice, thought and faith in your own capacity to attain enlightenment. Religions teach: God created the world; Implicate Technology teaches: conditioned existence unfolds, now, in the face of one unified unconditioned mind.

Now, through a religious or a secular teaching, you have a choice of paths to understanding reality. Reality is one: a glorious, glorious, glorious unity. All religions, and this secular teaching of Implicate Technology, are models of the one reality.

All models of reality are relevant, to a greater or lesser degree, to particular cultures over particular time periods. The relevance of this Implicate Technology model of reality can only be measured in terms of its effect on people's lives now. Your work with the Implicate Technology teachings, learning to live your life in harmony with the inherent implicate laws governing and informing all existence, will shape your contribution to the growth and development of our culture.

Bibliography

Chinese Taoism

Wilhelm, Richard and Jung, C. G.; *The Secret of the Golden Flower*; London, Routledge & Kegan Paul, 1962.
Chia, Mantak; *Awaken Healing Energy Through the Tao*; New York, Aurora Press, 1983.
Chia, Mantak; *Taoist Secrets of Love: Cultivating Male Sexual Energy*; New York, Aurora Press, 1984.

Tibetan Buddhism

Evans-Wentz, W. Y.; *The Tibetan Book of the Dead*; Oxford, Oxford University Press, 1960.
Evans-Wentz, W. Y.; *Tibet's Great Yogi Milarepa*; Oxford, Oxford University Press, 1969.
Evans-Wentz, W. Y.; *Tibetan Yoga and Secret Doctrines*; Oxford, Oxford University Press, 1967.
Evans-Wentz, W. Y.; *The Tibetan Book of the Great Liberation*; Oxford, Oxford University Press, 1968.
Govinda, Lama Anagarika; *Foundations of Tibetan Mysticism*; London, Rider, 1969.

Indian Hinduism

Shearer, Alexander; *Effortless Being: the Yoga Sutras of Patanjali*; London, Wildwood House, 1982.
Godman, David; *Be As You Are: the Teachings of Sri Ramana Maharshi*; London, Arkana, 1985.

Jewish Kabbalah

Hoffman, Edward; *The Way of Splendour: Jewish Mysticism and Modern Psychology*; Boulder, Shambhala, 1981.

Western Scientific Model of Reality

Bohm, David; *Wholeness and the Implicate Order*; London, Ark Paperbacks, 1983.

Glossary

Centred in the midst of conditions: the state of mind, achieved through the daily practice of **meditation**, which marks the start of the process of learning to understand the true nature of **reality**.

Clear setting face to face with reality: the experience of understanding the true nature of **reality**.

Conditions: the ten conditions which interact spontaneously to create each moment.

Enlightenment: the progressive states of awareness which, stage by stage, sweep aside ignorance of the nature of **reality**. Enlightenment culminates in the complete integration of the individual with all of **reality**.

Explicate: referring to aspects of **reality** which can be understood by the five senses.

Implicate: referring to aspects of **reality** which can only be understood by the sixth sense, or intuition.

Implicate technology: 1) The generic name for the underlying structure and practical techniques for expanding awareness, common to all fully-developed, spiritually based **models of reality**.
2) A practical technique, the correct use of which enables the individual to understand and integrate with the **implicate** aspects of **reality**.

Implicate Technology: 1) A Western-originated, structured meditative system, incorporating meditative techniques which work in a secular, everyday context.
2) A fully-developed, spiritually based Western **model of reality**.

Karma: 1) An inherent, implacable, **implicate** law of **reality**.
2) The process whereby **reality** structures the circumstances of your life, to guide you in understanding your own nature.
3) The law whereby your current thoughts and actions determine your future experience.

Meaning of life: 1) The ultimate experience, impossible to convey in words.
2) The understanding which arises when the final stage of **enlightenment** is realised.

Meditation: 1) The practical process of stilling the mind.
2) The self-help technique enabling you to reach **enlightenment**.
3) A practical technique which awakens the sixth sense, or intuition.

Model of reality: A structured, coherent description of **reality**, which uses practical techniques enabling the individual to experience the unity of **reality**.

Personality: the complex of views, opinions, ideas, emotions and attitudes comprising ordinary, everyday awareness. This complex is experienced as real to ordinary, everyday consciousness, relatively real once the first stage of **enlightenment** has been attained and relatively illusory once the final stage of **enlightenment** has been realised.

Power discipline: 1) A smooth, harmonious action in three steps: Input, Pivot then Act.
2) A mental tool to aid in the process of finding a harmonious and unselfish resolution to any difficult situation.

Power structure: 1) A way of describing how power is structured in any situation.
2) A way of understanding who controls, what is controlled, how it is controlled and why.

Purpose of life: 1) To understand the **meaning of life**.
2) The process of attaining **enlightenment**.

Reality: the total of what can be known and experienced. The true nature of reality can only be understood once the final stage of **enlightenment** has been realised.

Sexual energy: 1) The body's spontaneously generated **implicate** power source. Sexual energy is squandered in unenlightened sexual activity.
2) The power inherent in the psycho-physiological system which is refined and transmuted, consciously or unconsciously, in advanced meditative activity.

Synopsis of Contents

Live
Live the teachings,
live the teachings.

Act
Act according to your intuition.
Don't interfere.
Just let things happen.

The formula for attaining enlightenment is:

Throughout your life, Live and Act